FATHER

MW00801073

Our Lady of Good Help

Mary's Message and Mission for Adele Brise and the World

Amor DEUS PUBLISHING

Our Lady of Good Help:
Mary's Message and Mission for Adele Brise and the World
Father Edward Looney

Cover image: Shutterstock.com
Cover and book design: Amor Deus Publishing Design Department

Imprimatur granted on April 25, 2013 by The Most Reverend David L. Ricken, DD, JCL, Bishop of Green Bay

Nihil Obstat granted by Reverend Alfred McBride, O. Praem

For information regarding permission, write to:
Amor Deus Publishing
Attention: Permissions Dept.
4727 North 12th Street
Phoenix, AZ 85014

ISBN 978-1-61956-125-0

Second Edition June 2014
10 9 8 7 6 5 4 3 2

Published and printed in the United States of America by Amor Deus Publishing, an imprint of Vesuvius Press Incorporated.
For additional inspirational books visit us at AmorDeus.com

DEDICATION

In 2005, at the age of 16, my life was changed by a Marian pilgrimage led by a woman from my parish, Joyce Lightner. My Marian fire was ignited at that young age and continues to this day. It was with great sadness that I learned of Joyce's passing during the summer of 2012 while abroad studying Spanish. In gratitude for her love and devotion of leading pilgrims to Jesus through Mary, I dedicate this book to her memory. May her soul and the souls of all the faithful departed, through the mercy of God, rest in peace.

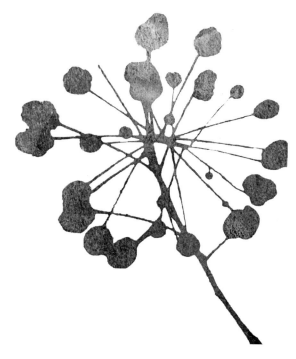

A SPECIAL ACKNOWLEDGMENT:

This book is the fruit of research undertaken for a paper presentation given at the 2011 meeting of the Mariological Society of America (MSA) in Scottsdale, Arizona. The original paper was entitled "Called to Evangelize: The Story of Sister Adele Brise," and served as inspiration for the first two parts of this book. I am grateful to the MSA for allowing me to reproduce parts of my presentation in this book.

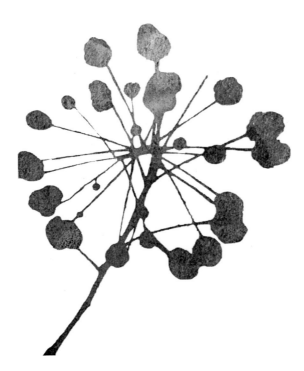

TABLE OF CONTENTS:

PART III: UNDERSTANDING CHAMPION IN LIGHT OF APPROVED MARIAN APPARITIONS

DISCLAIMER:

The value of private revelations is essentially different from that of the one public revelation: the latter demands faith; in it God himself speaks to us through human words and the mediation of the living community of the Church. The criterion for judging the truth of a private revelation is its orientation to Christ himself. If it leads us away from him, then it certainly does not come from the Holy Spirit, who guides us more deeply into the gospel, and not away from it. Private revelation is an aid to this faith, and it demonstrates its credibility precisely because it refers back to the one public revelation. **Ecclesiastical approval of a private revelation** essentially means that its message contains nothing contrary to faith and morals; it is licit to make it public and the faithful are authorized to give to it their prudent adhesion. A private revelation can introduce new emphases, give rise to new forms of piety, or deepen older ones. It can have a certain prophetic character (cf. *1 Th* 5:19-21) and can be a valuable aid for better understanding and living the gospel at a certain time; consequently it should not be treated lightly. **It is a help which is proffered, but its use is not obligatory.** In any event, it must be a matter of nourishing faith, hope and love, which are for everyone the permanent path of salvation.

From the Preface of *Norms regarding the manner of proceeding in the discernment of presumed apparitions or revelations* written by William Cardinal Levada. Available through the Vatican Website:
http://www.vatican.va/roman_curia/congregations/cfaith/documents/rc_con_cfaith_doc_20111214_prefazione-levada_en.html

Nota Bene: **(Emphasis added)**

PART I:
UNDERSTANDING ADELE'S LIFE AND MARY'S NAME, MESSAGE, AND MISSION

In his presidential address at the 43rd meeting of the Mariological Society of America, Fr. James McCurry, OFM Conv. proposed that Our Lady of Guadalupe was the evangelizer of the Americas.[1] In his paper, he argued a Guadalupan formula for evangelization emphasizing three aspects: the Blessed Virgin's name, her message, and her mission. As McCurry applied these three aspects of evangelization to the Guadalupan apparition, this first part will present a historical analysis of the apparition in light of Mary's name, message, and mission as revealed to Sister Adele Brise.

By categorizing the dialogue Adele had with Mary using Fr. McCurry's analysis of Guadalupe, the message and mission received by Adele, although personal, and the mission, although entrusted first to Adele, should be embraced by all those who read, hear, or visit the Shrine of Our Lady of Good Help. In terms of this Mariophany (an apparition of Mary), it is necessary to make the distinction between personal message and mission. The questions Our Lady asked Adele were of a personal nature but when taken out of the context of being addressed to Adele, the personal aspect meant for Adele, can also deepen an individual's personal introspection of their Christian life.

In order to understand the analysis given in this book, it would be best for the text of Adele's conversation with Mary to be reproduced. The dialogue was quite simple but at the same time very deep.

'In God's name, who are you and what do you want of me?' asked Adele, as she had been directed.

'I am the Queen of Heaven, who prays for the

---

1   Fr. James McCurry, OFM Conv., "Our Lady of Guadalupe: Evangelizer of the Americas," *Marian Studies* XLIII (1992): 9-16.

conversion of sinners, and I wish you to do the same. You received Holy Communion this morning, and that is well. But you must do more. Make a general confession, and offer Communion for the conversion of sinners. If they do not convert and do penance, my Son will be obliged to punish them'

'Adele, who is it?" said one of the women. 'O why can't we see her as you do?' said another weeping. 'Kneel,' said Adele, 'the Lady says she is the Queen of Heaven.'

Our Blessed Lady turned, looked kindly at them, and said, **'Blessed are they that believe without seeing. What are you doing here in idleness...while your companions are working in the vineyard of my Son?'**

'What more can I do, dear Lady?' said Adele, weeping.

'Gather the children in this wild country and teach them what they should know for salvation.'

'But how shall I teach them who know so little myself?' replied Adele.

'Teach them,' *replied her radiant visitor,* **'their catechism, how to sign themselves with the sign of the Cross, and how to approach the sacraments; that is what I wish you to do. Go and fear nothing. I will help you.'**[2]

Nota Bene: **Bold text** indicates the spoken words of Our Lady

---

2   Sister M. Dominica, OSF, *The Chapel: Our Lady of Good Help* (DePere: Journal Publishing Co, 1955), 8-9.

CHAPTER 1:
A PERSONAL MESSAGE

A number of years ago, prior to the 2010 approval of Adele's Mariophany, the story of Adele's apparition was relayed to a priest who serves in the Archdiocese of Milwaukee. Although he served at a parish in Milwaukee, he had never heard of the Shrine of Our Lady of Good Help, even though it was only 2 hours north. After hearing the story, he said something striking, perhaps unsettling at first, but after reflecting on it, one can see the truth in his statement. He believed the apparition to Adele was of a personal nature, meant only for her. Using the Guadalupan analysis of Fr. James McCurry, one could rightly analyze the message and even the mission of the apparition as being solely for Adele. Even though the poignant questions related to her personal life, the underlying principle of the question could still be applied to anyone who hears Adele's story.

Within the brief dialogue between Mary and Adele, Mary asked a particularly poignant question: "What are you doing here in idleness while your companions are working the vineyard of my Son?" This question struck a chord within Adele's heart because it brought her back to her early life in Belgium, forcing her to reflect upon her current state in life. As a young child, Adele had an ardent desire to enter the religious life. She was instructed by a religious community of sisters as a young child in preparation for her first Holy Communion, and it is reported that "[s]he and several of her companions had promised our Lady at that time to become religious and devote their lives to the foreign missions. The other girls followed their vocation."[1] Prior to her parents' immigration to the United States, Adele was troubled about leaving Belgium because of the pact she made so many years earlier with her friends. Her confessor, however, told her to go with her parents to America and added, "If God wills it, you will become a Sister in America. Go, I will pray for you."[2] At

---

[1] Dominica, 10.
[2] Dominica, 10.

the age of 24 (in 1855), Adele boarded a ship bound for America with her family, not as a religious sister but as a lay woman.

Her childhood promise was to join a community of sisters so she could work in the foreign missions. Upon her arrival in the United States, Adele was an immigrant in a foreign land. Not sent by a religious community, but instead through the will of her parents. In the years leading up to 1859 Adele could have fulfilled that childhood promise by joining an order of sisters in the United States. Instead, she dedicated her life to the settlement and worked for her family "in the fields, preparing the soil for planting with the most primitive tools, carrying grain on their heads to the grist mill a distance of many miles, and preparing shingles for market."[3] The question Mary asked Adele was personal, it struck her heart because as Our Lady said, she was idle while her companions were working in the vineyard of the Lord.

Reflecting upon Adele's early life, one can then understand the question the Blessed Mother posed, but for the person who reads, hears, and heeds the mission given to Adele Brise, one might ask, how does this question apply to me? While it is true this question was of a personal nature, it applies to all who hear the message. How often are we idle? We spend countless hours surfing the Internet or watching endless hours of television, forfeiting time spent in prayer, reflection, or availing ourselves of the sacraments. By no means are we to forego recreation, as it is an essential part of one's livelihood, nevertheless, one should not recreate to excess at the expense of the spiritual. These questions call us to do something more. It calls us to go beyond ourselves.

Yes, Adele received a personal message when asked why she was standing in idleness. It was a question with a number of presuppositions pertaining to Adele's early childhood, yet the question posed to her can be posed to us. Instead of remaining idle, we too can participate in Adele's contemplative and active mission. We are left to ask ourselves, when is the last time I prayed for the conversion of sinners? When is the last time I went to the Sacrament of Penance? How often do I go to Mass? Do I spend time in prayer daily? Do I read the bible? How do I teach my children or grandchildren or support my parish's youth? These questions force us to reflect on our own state in

---

3   Dominica, 5.

life, just as Adele had to do in 1859. Adele found her primary vocation in life through her dialogue with Mary. Although we will never receive our vocation like she did, we can, however, be inspired by those who have gone before us. The saints inspire us to live holier lives. Although not canonized, Adele Brise and her mission of prayer and catechesis should be no exception.

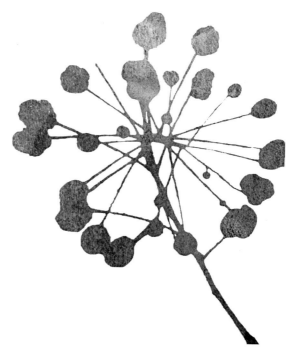

CHAPTER 2:
THE CONTEMPLATIVE MISSION

After an initial read-through of Adele's dialogue with Mary coupled with the extensive newspaper coverage emphasizing the apparition's catechetical aspect, it is relatively easy to overlook the first part of Mary's mission to Adele. It is true, Mary did tell Adele to gather the children and teach them their catechism – a task to which she dedicated her entire life, but Our Lady spoke of prayer and the sacraments from the very beginning. Mary was relaying to Adele a mission of prayer, which could be characterized as a contemplative aspect of the mission.

In the first week of October, culminating on October 9, 1859, Adele received a total of three apparitions. While carrying grain to the local grist mill, Adele saw a beautiful woman standing between a maple and a hemlock tree for the first time.[1] Adele saw a woman dressed in white who said nothing and quickly departed, leaving a cloud behind.[2] Adele returned home, and unlike other Marian visionaries,[3] Adele's family did not dismiss her claims but suggested that it may have been a soul from purgatory in need of prayers. They encouraged Adele to pray for the souls in purgatory.

On the following Sunday, October 9, Adele left her home with Isabelle, her sister, and a local neighbor woman[4] for the ten-mile journey to the church. It is interesting to note that Adele was not accompanied by her parents, Lambert and Catherine, but by her sister and the neighbor, begging the question of whether or not her family practiced their faith since arriving from Belgium. Rev. John Perrodin, a clergyman who visited the settlement from time to time, wrote of the Belgian people's spiritual crisis because they lacked a pastor who could care for their spiritual and

---

1   The date of this apparition is unknown, but we know that it did precede October 9.

2   Dominica, 7.

3   Bernadette at Lourdes was met with speculation; the same was true for the Fatima children. It is probable that given Adele's age (28), she was easier to believe than a young child.

4   She remains unnamed and unidentified although there is speculation as to her identity.

sacramental needs.[5] Had Lambert and Catherine fallen prey to that spiritual crisis? Did Adele remain a faithful Catholic because of her childhood desire to join a religious order? It is possible her parents may have attended Mass earlier in the morning, but one must keep in mind at this time in the Church there were no Saturday Vigil Masses, and the faithful were required to fast until the *ite missa est* (the dismissal at Mass). There is no definite answer to this question, and any conclusion is only speculative, but given Our Lady's mission of prayer for the conversion of sinners, we can ask, was it hitting close to home for Adele? We do know her parents believed the miraculous happenings, and following the apparition Lambert built the first chapels on the property with assistance from local townspeople.

On the morning of October 9, on the way to Mass, Adele approached the same location where she had seen the woman dressed in white, and again she saw the same woman. Like the first time, she did not speak to Adele and quickly vanished. Adele's companions knew she was afraid and that something was wrong, but she gathered enough strength to continue to the church.[6] Following Mass, Adele spoke with Fr. Verhoef, recounting the two earlier visions and asked what she should do if the visitor returned. He instructed her to pose the following question to the woman: "In God's name, who are you and what do you want of me?" It appeared that the visitor would only speak upon Adele's initiative. Later that day, approaching the same spot, Adele saw the woman again. Armed with the question, Adele began a conversation, by the end of which she would be instructed to undertake a mission of prayer and catechesis. Of particular importance was Mary's identification and her conveyance of a contemplative (prayerful) mission to Adele.

Our Lady said, "I am the Queen of Heaven, who prays for the conversion of sinners, and I wish you to do the same." Mary identified herself as an intercessor, one who prays for others. This task of intercession was not restricted to the Mother of God alone, but she wanted Adele to do the same. As soon as Mary identified herself, she entrusted Adele with a mission distinct from catechesis – she was to pray for the conversion of sinners. Secondly, Our Lady commended Adele for her reception of Holy

---

5   Dominica, 3.

6   Dominica, 8.

Communion at Mass earlier that morning. Besides reception of Holy Communion, Adele had to do more; she was instructed to make a general confession and to offer her Communion for the conversion of sinners.

Our Lady was instructing Adele to engage her spiritual life before undertaking the active mission of catechizing young people. The implication of Mary giving a contemplative and active mission shows the importance of spiritual preparation for any mission. Before Adele could go out and instruct the children in the Catholic faith, she first had to prepare herself spiritually and sacramentally. Before working for the conversion of sinners, she had to pray for those for whom she would work to convert through instruction. In addition, she had to amend her life and repent of her own sins by seeking absolution in the Sacrament of Penance. The Eucharist and Penance were the two wellsprings from which Adele could draw her strength, the stream of grace to which she could return daily in order to fully achieve her active mission of catechesis. Adele's active mission had to be preceded by her own prayerful and sacramental preparation.

This contemplative mission, while unique to Adele's state in life and the mission she was to undertake, is relevant for all of us today. We are to join the Blessed Virgin Mary in her intercession for the conversion of sinners. We must receive the Eucharist worthily and go to confession. The Lord calls and invites people today to participate in Adele's mission, but in order to be effective messengers of God's Word, we must go to the Lord in prayer and return to the sacraments of the Church. We must live what we teach. People will only listen to us if we practice what we preach. If you desire your family to go to confession or Mass more often, instead of simply telling them, allow them to witness your own belief in the sacraments and invite them to join you. The contemplative mission entrusted to Adele was a universal mission for all who hear the message – pray for the conversion of sinners, go to confession, and receive the Eucharist. By doing these three things, you will work to fulfill the contemplative aspect of Adele's mission, which she faithfully fulfilled throughout her entire life.

CHAPTER 3

THE ACTIVE MISSION

In chapter one, Mary's question about Adele's idleness was addressed, as well as how it related to her early childhood desire to become a religious sister. In response to the question, Adele asked, "What more can I do, dear Lady?"[1] What more could Adele do? She was told to "[g]ather the children in this wild country and teach them what they should know for salvation. [...] Teach them their catechism, how to sign themselves with the Sign of the Cross, and how to approach the sacraments."[2] Adele was to become an active missionary among the Belgian immigrants; as such, this mission could be characterized as an active mission. In most Catholic writing, the mission of catechesis is what has popularized Our Lady's apparition to Adele. The question of Adele's idleness after having immigrated to America has been answered. No longer should Adele remain idle, but she must dedicate herself to this mission of gathering the children and teaching them the faith. Adele faithfully dedicated her life to this mission.

Adele's early method of evangelization spanned the course of seven years, traveling up to fifty miles from home through all types of weather. Walking from village to village, knocking on doors, she offered to do housework for families in exchange for permission to teach their children what the Queen of Heaven had prescribed. Walking from home to home at great distances, one could easily imagine how exhausted Adele became. Impressed with her piety and willingness to follow her calling to these extremes, Fr. Phillip Crud, the newly appointed pastor to the Belgian colony, encouraged Adele to begin a life that others could share in order to fulfill her mission. With a letter from her pastor, Adele set out with a companion to begin the first of many begging missions throughout the settlement.

Supported by others, Adele began a lay third order group of

---

1   Dominica, 9.
2   Dominica, 9.

sisters, often called the Sisters of Good Health, but whom Adele called the Sisters of St. Francis of Assisi.[3] Over the years, many young women joined the group for a short time. This group enjoyed recognition by the Diocese of Green Bay, and as such, they wore a religious habit and referred to each other as "Sister."[4] Taking no formal vows, they were free to leave whenever they wished. In the late 1860s the Sisters of St. Francis of Assisi were instrumental in founding St. Mary's Academy, distinguished as the second school in the diocese. The sisters taught in both French and English, and Adele was responsible for the students' religious formation, often orphans and other children who were sent there to have a better life.

Adele took her responsibilities seriously. When she felt the students were prepared for admission to the sacraments, she would present them to the pastor who would examine and admit them to Holy Communion.[5] Adele's active mission was specifically meant for her, but it also can be seen as a universal call. Her call to catechesis forces us to discern how we are called to participate in the work of evangelization and catechesis today, whether it is in a parish setting or from within our own home or family.

---

3   Dominica, 16. Many people erroneously refer to the shrine as the Shrine of Our Lady of Good Health. Sister Dominica text acknowledges this as a common problem.

4   In a letter dated December 10, 1895 obtained from the Diocesan archives, Bishop Joseph Fox referred to Adele as "Soeur Adele."

5   Dominica, 10.

CHAPTER 4

NOTRE DAME DE BON SECOURS

The Names of Mary

The chapel erected on the site of Mary's appearance to Adele for over a century has been called the Chapel (now the Shrine) of Our Lady of Good Help. The shrine's name is unique since Mary identified herself as the Queen of Heaven who prays for the conversion of sinners. Mary came as a queen to encourage sinners to repent through her message to Adele. Mary made it clear she wanted all souls to be saved for her Son's sake. As she prays for the conversion of sinners, she gives Adele an instruction to catechize, which facilitates conversion because in this way we are given the ways to convert, do penance, and amend our lives.

Understanding the name "Queen of Heaven" sheds some light in understanding the second name applied to Mary at Champion, which came through Adele's devotional life. Similar to the Polish devotion to Our Lady of Czestochowa or the Hispanic devotion to Our Lady of Guadalupe, the Belgian people had a culturally-derived devotion to Mary under the title of *Notre Dame de Bon Secours* (Our Lady of Good Help), in which a confraternity with specific prayers and litanies existed.[1] With her devotion already cultivated, Adele had chapels in Champion[2] dedicated under the title Our Lady of Good Help. Fittingly enough, Mary promised to assist Adele in her catechetical mission by her departing words, "[G]o and fear nothing, I will help you." Adele often relied on the help and intercession of the Blessed Mother in her begging missions, during the Peshtigo fire, and in the defeat of heresy. As news of the apparition spread, people began to flock to the small chapel, seeking Mary's aid. Adele's devotion to *Notre Dame de Bon Secours* could be because she took inspiration from St. Marguerite Bourgeoys, who founded the Sisters of Notre-Dame as a teaching order and built a chapel in honor of *Notre Dame*

---

1   C.f. Confraternity of Our Lady of Good Help, *Regles de la Confrerie de Notre-Dame de Bon-Secours*, (Mons : Imp. de Masquillier et Lamir, 1778).

2   At the time, the village was known in common parlance as Robinsonville.

de Bon Secours.[3] Given St. Marguerite's devotion to Mary under this title, we find the devotion dates to at least the mid-1600s.[4] Regardless of the reasons for Adele's decision to have the chapel dedicated under this title, the Lady of Good Help surely acted as an intercessor in the work of evangelization and catechesis as Adele strove to bring people closer to Jesus so they could reach Heaven.

Help in the Mission

Adele believed in the mission she was given – to pray and work for the conversion of souls. As a result, Adele undertook a lot of work for the sake of the mission. Immediately following the apparition, for seven years Adele walked throughout the peninsula, going from home to home, doing small household chores in exchange for teaching the children. She entrusted her health and safety to Mary. In the early days of the tertiary sisters' establishment, Adele had to beg for money. In the beginning, there was

> [n]o price for teaching, no tuition bills... Then this courageous woman undertook to beg, from more favored communities, the money necessary for building a large school-house, then a Chapel, and, finally to raise a home for the religious, whom she hoped to persuade to assist her in her great work.[5]

Adele relied on the help of people from the community in order for the mission to be completed. At times, the sisters were uncertain

---

3   Marguerite Bourgeoys (1620-1700) - Biography," Vatican: The Holy See, http://www.vatican.va/news_services/liturgy/saints/ns_lit_doc_19821031_bourgeoys_en.html (accessed March 26, 2011).

4   The devotion to Our Lady of Good Help was renewed by Bishop Ignace Bourget, the Bishop of Montreal, who sought to restore devotion and pilgrimages to the Chapel of Our Lady of Good Help in response to a terrible epidemic. He cited Our Lady of Good Help as one who can help to destroy error and vice, especially drunkenness and impurity. Furthermore, in his pastoral letter, the bishop erected a confraternity to Our Lady of Good Help and established the titular feast of Our Lady of Good Help as May 24. To read the letter, see: Fr. Xavier Donald MacLeod, *History of the Devotion to the Blessed Virgin Mary in North America* (New York: Virtue & Yorston, 1966), 326-337.

5   Dominica, 13.

what [they] would have for breakfast. When that occurred, Sister Adele would gather her companions after the children were in bed and repair [sic] to the Chapel to beg Mary's help. Before morning someone would invariably drop off a bag of flour or a supply of meat at their door. Many of the boarders brought supplies from home as a means of compensation.[6]

The sisters continually relied on divine providence, which could be considered Mary's intercession for the sake of the mission. Their devotion and reliance upon *Notre Dame de Bon Secours* and Mary's constant intercession is evident by Adele's complete trust in God.

The Peshtigo Fire

On the eve of the twelfth anniversary of the apparition, a horrific event unfolded in Northeastern Wisconsin. During an extended drought, fire broke out in the small lumber village of Peshtigo.[7] Igniting on the same day as the more infamous Great Chicago Fire, the Peshtigo Fire has been described as the most devastating fire in the history of the United States.[8] Fr. Peter Pernin, an eyewitness in Peshtigo on October 8, 1871, told how some survived that terrible day by taking refuge in the Peshtigo River and "turning [their hearts] towards heaven as their only resource."[9] The fire tornado that began in Peshtigo then leaped across the bay and penetrated the Door Peninsula;[10] next in its path of destruction was Robinsonville, where Adele, her sisters, and the wooden Chapel of Our Lady of Good Help stood in its way.

People in the Door Peninsula, particularly the area surrounding the Belgian settlement, were unaware of the happenings in Peshtigo. When the ferocious whirlwinds of

---

6   Dominica, 13-14.

7   Fr. Peter Pernin, *The Great Peshtigo Fire: An Eyewitness Account (Wisconsin)*, 2nd ed. (Madison: Wisconsin Historical Society, 1999), 16-18.

8   Martin W. Sandler, *Lost to Time: Unforgettable Stories That History Forgot* (New York, NY.: Sterling, 2010), 181.

9   Pernin, 42.

10   It could also be argued that given the conditions throughout the state, another fire broke out in the region. Such an argument would have to be researched in light of meteorological data for October 8, 1871.

explosive heat and flame overtook the territory, they too believed that the end of the world was upon them.[11] The people of the area, staring death in the eye, took refuge at the Chapel of Our Lady of Good Help. Trusting in Our Lady's intercession, they begged for aid. Adele was "determined not to abandon Mary's shrine. [...] [T]he children, the Sisters, and the farmers with their families ... drove their livestock before them and raced in the direction of Mary's sanctuary."[12] The chapel had become filled with

> terror stricken people beseeching the Mother of God to spare them, many wailing aloud in their fright. Filled with confidence, they entered the chapel, reverently raised the statue of Mary, and kneeling, bore it in procession around their beloved sanctuary. When the wind and fire exposed them to suffocation, they turned in another direction and continued to hope and pray, saying the rosary.[13]

Praying for many hours outside of the wooden chapel (which by its very composition should have been incinerated), the people found relief in the early hours of October 9, the day commemorating Adele's message. Rain eventually fell, extinguishing the fire.[14] Our Lady of Good Help had answered the people's prayers.

Fr. Pernin, after hearing of the chapel's miraculous preservation, journeyed to Robinsonville (Champion) to see for himself. In the original manuscript, entitled "The Finger of God," he recounted that

> [a]ll the houses and fences in the neighborhood had been burned, with the exception of the school, the chapel, and fences surrounding the six acres of land consecrated to the Blessed Virgin... [the property] sanctified by the visible presence of the Mother of God now shone out like an emerald island amid a sea of ashes.[15]

---

11   Dominica, 19.

12   Dominica, 19.

13   Dominica, 19.

14   Dominica, 20.

15   Peter Pernin, *The Finger of God*, an unpublished manuscript accessed through the

The chapel stood as a testament to God's miraculous intervention through His Holy Mother's intercession. Trusting in Mary's assurance of help, people believed that God could and would spare them through the Blessed Virgin's intercession.

The Old Catholic Heresy

The physical threat to the chapel was soon overshadowed by a spiritual threat. Fr. Joseph Vilatte, a baptized Catholic, left the Church and was ordained a priest for the Old Catholic Church. He moved to the Belgian territory and began seeking to gain converts. The Old Catholic Church was formed in the late 1800s by Catholics who did not accept papal infallibility. As such, the Old Catholic Church denied the Immaculate Conception, confession, and indulgences; it also viewed clerical celibacy as optional and celebrated Mass in the vernacular.[16]

During his time in Wisconsin, Vilatte took up residence in the town of Duvall, where he erected an Old Catholic Church between two Catholic churches.[17] Due to the number of people flocking to his sect, Adele became concerned with the loss of souls and so faithfully prayed that he would do no more harm and return to the Catholic Church. Bishop Messmer became aware of the growing heresy in the Peninsula and invited Fr. Pennings and the Canons Regular of Premontre, commonly referred to as the Norbertines, from Berne Abbey in Holland to the diocese to combat this heresy. In 1895, Fr. Pennings began an annual pilgrimage to the chapel "to beseech Mary's help against the evil work and influence of Vilatte" and to catechize the settlers.[18] The Old Catholic Church was unable to flourish in the Door Peninsula because Catholics who might have been drawn to the sect were unwilling to accept implementation of their reforms, especially public confession and the abolition of Mary's cult.[19] Vilatte's failure to gain converts to Old Catholicism in Wisconsin led him elsewhere, but by the end of his life, he had confessed his wrongdoing and displayed remorse for having led approximately 500,000 Catholics astray and returned to the

---

Shrine of Our Lady of Good Help archives.

16   Dominica, 24.

17   Dominica, 24.

18   Dominica, 25.

19   Dominica, 26.

Catholic Church. After recanting his heretical beliefs, he took up a life of penance at the Cistercian Abbey of Pon-Colbert in Versailles, France, where he died as a layman.[20]

Vilatte's bid to evangelize and convert people to Old Catholicism had been preempted by the Blessed Mother. Her triumph over heresy was marked in the end by faithful people who could not forego their Marian piety. Vilatte's conversion marked another milestone in Adele's life. As in 1871, when the faithful had gathered with her in prayer at the chapel to spare their land, Adele's prayers were answered (after her death) for Vilatte's conversion and the demise of the heretical sect. The name of Mary as the Queen of Heaven and her role of interceding for the conversion of sinners were realized in Vilatte's conversion, just as Mary's intercession had prevented the spread of heresy.

Miraculous Cures[21]

Since the apparitions, many people have claimed that they were cured as a result of a visit to the apparition site. At the preserved site of the apparition crutches, canes, and braces have been left behind by those who were once crippled yet who could walk again as a result of their visit. Sister Dominica relays several miracle accounts ranging from a person hard of hearing being able to hear without a hearing aid to a blind child who was granted sight.[22] In November 2010, a family from Green Bay claimed that their three-year-old child had been cured of leukemia as a result of visiting the shrine.[23] The Shrine of Our Lady of Good Help has been a place of intercession, where pilgrims have turned in times of need. Regardless of whether or not petitions were answered in the way pilgrims desired, the Blessed Mother surely interceded to the Triune God for their intentions.

---

20   Msgr. Joseph Marx, "Vilatte and the Catholic Church," *The Salesianum* 37, no. 3 (July 1942): 113-20.

21   No cure or healing attributed to the intercession of Our Lady at the Shrine of Our Lady of Good Help has ever been formally investigated or verified.

22   Dominica, 26-7.

23   Sam Lucero, "Family says visit to shrine cured boy's leukemia", *The Compass*, 17 February 2011, http://thecompassnews.org/news/local/1981-family-says-visit-to-shrine-cured-boys-leukemia.html

Our Lady of Good Help

While the name "Our Lady of Good Help" has no tangible relationship to the apparition's message besides Mary's promise of help to Adele, this is the name that has been commonly associated with the Shrine. From the very beginning Adele had chapels dedicated to Mary under this title. Her devotion to Our Lady of Good Help was fitting, given her life experiences and the shrine's history. Adele relied so often on Mary's intercession with her Son. The miraculous preservation of the property and those gathered at the chapel on that horrific day in 1871 shows Mary's protection over the ground she hallowed by her presence twelve years earlier. The defeat and conversion of Joseph Vilatte could also be attributed to the Queen of Heaven. Lastly, like any apparition site throughout the world, pilgrims come with their special intentions in hopes that the Mother of God will intercede for them. The Shrine of Our Lady of Good Help is a visible testament and monument to the power of Mary's intercessory role in the life of the Church. The shrine testifies to the fact that Mary intervened in Adele's life, calling her to a life of prayer and catechesis which led to the foundation of a school and tertiary order of lay Franciscan sisters. It has been a place that has stood the test of time and threats, and so Our Lady's message is still being heard, heeded, and honored today by the countless pilgrims who daily visit the shrine.

CHAPTER 5:
IF THEY DO NOT CONVERT

There are some people who do not accept Marian apparitions, because if they were real, they would have to change their life; they would have to convert, do penance, and amend their life. Truth be told, no one has to accept the stories of Mary's apparitions as they are only private revelation, and not a part of the public revelation of the Church. Private revelation has a tendency to make people uncomfortable because it challenges complacency. Because of this, apparitions sometimes are quickly dismissed, approved or not.

At a conference an individual challenged the veracity of the apparition because of the so-called chastisement language, which she associated with the natural disaster theory of chastisement. Our Lady told Adele, "If they do not convert and do penance, my Son will be obliged to punish them." Many people find themselves troubled by such startling statements because we understand God as a loving Father who would not inflict serious punishment on His children. This could arguably be challenged by biblical examples specifically from Genesis – the punishment of Original Sin and the Great Flood (Gen. 6-9). Yet one could respond that God promised not to destroy the world again, and the rainbow in Gen. 9:11 signified that. However, the Genesis narrative indicates God will not destroy the world by a flood again; it says nothing about a different type of possible future destruction. The Old Testament prophets also spoke of conversion and amendment of life in order to prevent destruction. Another understanding of God's punishment (or discipline) can be derived from Hebrews 12 where the author writes:

> My son, do not disdain the discipline of the Lord or lose heart when reproved by Him; for whom the Lord loves, He disciplines; He scourges every son He acknowledges. Endure your trials as "discipline"; God treats you as sons. For what "son" is there whom his father does not discipline? If you are without discipline, in which all

have shared, you are not sons but bastards. Besides this, we have had our earthly fathers to discipline us, and we respected them. Should we not [then] submit all the more to the Father of spirits and live? They disciplined us for a short time as seemed right to them, but He does so for our benefit, in order that we may share His holiness. At the time, all discipline seems a cause not for joy but for pain, yet later it brings the peaceful fruit of righteousness to those who are trained by it.[1]

There is a tendency to view chastisement language as negative. The author of Hebrews, however, tells us the Father disciplines us so that we can grow in holiness. God loves His children so much that He wishes for them to return to Him. The Father desires the return of His prodigal children who confess, "Father, I have sinned against heaven and against you; I no longer deserve to be called your son" (Luke 15:21 NAB). The Father desires to embrace His son and throw a feast because His son, who once was dead, is alive again. The Lord desires conversion and amendment of life; that is why Mary prays for the conversion of sinners; that is why Adele was to do the same; that was why Adele was to work vigorously for the salvation of souls through catechesis.

One could easily look at the Peshtigo Fire and note it happened twelve years after the apparition and was thus the chastisement "prophesied" by Mary to Adele. Sister Dominica in her historical account of the apparition states, "We do not propose to pass judgment on the reasons for this catastrophe, but we know that twelve years later almost to the day, October 8, 1871, the great calamity fell," but she does suggest "the Lord used the forces of nature to accomplish His ends."[2] While Adele appears never to have confirmed the Peshtigo Fire as fulfilling Our Lady's prophesy of a chastisement, the fire did have an effect upon Adele's claims. The chapel's preservation from the fire was attributed to Our Lady's intervention. This was seen in direct correlation to Adele's claim to have seen Our Lady at that spot. Since then, no other explanation for the "miracle" has been proffered, and belief in the apparitions has taken root in the

---

1   Hebrews 12:5-11. (NAB)

2   Dominica, 17.

mind of the local people.

There are two alternative views one could potentially hold while not subscribing directly to the natural calamity theory of chastisement (viewed in light of the Peshtigo Fire). Our Lady told Adele that there is a pressing need for individuals to convert; otherwise, punishment would result. Sin in itself brings consequences; thus, the punishment could be seen as a result of a particular sin.[3] This theory plays out in various ways in contemporary society. For example, abortion or contraception brings with it the consequence of possible sterilization. In vitro fertilization may cause the conception and birth of twins, triplets, quintuplets, etc. when only one child was desired. Lying brings about the consequence of the truth being discovered. Whether revealed by God in the scriptures or through the mediation of the Church, whenever we attempt to play God and make decisions contrary to His laws, it seems there are negative consequences associated with that particular decision (or sin). While some of these contemporary examples probably were not prevalent in the late 1800s, the Peshtigo Fire arguably could be seen as a result of personal sins – namely greed. Despite the little rainfall that year, people continued to work to the detriment of their safety, clearing and burning the fields. They were concerned with producing and selling lumber instead of their own personal safety. Thus, the fire could be seen as a result of negligence. Those who sought refuge at the chapel were spared as a result of their trust in Mary's intercession, as they turned to God in their hour of need and not themselves. From this theory then, the Peshtigo Fire is not seen as a punishment sent by God because the people had not heeded Our Lady's requests, but rather, the fire is seen as a result of selfishness – a consequence of people's sinfulness. Consequentially, another understanding can be found with this interpretation, namely that Jesus' judgment would be experienced upon death. If one was to heed Our Lady's request by converting their life, the judgment experienced would be reduced, had they not converted. This coincides well with Our Lady's zeal for the salvation of souls expressed to Adele Brise.

If these attempts of explaining Our Lady's words have not been satisfactory, perhaps yet another understanding may help.

---

3   This is not to say hurricanes or other calamites occur as a result of sin, but rather, consequences arise from the sin itself.

Keeping in continuity with the theme of analyzing the apparition in terms of a personal message and a universal mission, the message's "chastisement" element could be recognized as part of a personal message to Adele, similar to Mary's earlier question of "What are you doing here in idleness...?" Adele felt she was unworthy of carrying out the task Our Lady was entrusting to her. She said, "[B]ut what more can I do for I know so little myself?" Adele had received a meager education, was poor, and was blind in one eye. Her appearance was startling to many. Despite her unworthiness, it was Adele who was being entrusted with this mission. Perhaps Mary's startling question was meant to encourage Adele, to spur her on to faithfulness in carrying out the mission. If she did not pray for the conversion of sinners and work for that conversion by teaching, Mary's Son would have been obliged to punish them. In the English translation, the word used, "if," is a conditional.[4] *If* people did not convert and do penance, *then* punishment would follow. It was not guaranteed to happen, and one way to ensure that it did not would be Adele's tireless dedication to the task of prayer and catechesis. If Adele carried out her mission despite her unworthiness, lack of education, and handicap, there would be conversions, which would please God, and, it would seem, stay His wrath. Given that Adele faithfully prayed for conversions and worked tirelessly for that cause, would God have sent a chastisement (as in a natural disaster)? Or was the Peshtigo Fire a result of sin? Or was the 'chastisement' indicative of the natural consequences of sin (apart from the Peshtigo Fire)? These questions are open for discernment, but the main principle to be concluded from Our Lady's message is her desire for people to conform their lives to the gospel message of our Blessed Lord, who exhorted us to repent and believe in the gospel (Mark 1:15).

---

4   It is this author's opinion that Mary spoke to Adele in French because of the numerous accounts stating Adele did not speak English well and needed an interpreter when she embarked on her begging missions. Sister Dominica references Eliza Allen Starr, who stated in her book *Patron Saints* that only the youngest Sister could speak English. C.f. Dominica, 13.

CHAPTER 6:
ADELE'S MISSION IN
THE 20TH AND 21ST CENTURY

In 1896, when Adele was on her deathbed, she summoned a former student named Josie in order to encourage her to continue the work she had done. Adele told Josie to "be kind to the sick and the old, and continue to instruct the children in their religion as I have done."[1] In the years following Adele's death, the Shrine of Our Lady of Good Help[2] has carried out numerous apostolates which have continued Adele's mission. Throughout the years, these various ministries could be classified in light of the historical analysis presented in this book, in light of Adele's contemplative and active mission. Adele's mission did not die with her in 1896 but lived on through various people who have responded to the call of Our Lord and Blessed Lady to pray for sinners and to catechize the young and the old. It is a mission that continues to this very day.

The Contemplative Mission
In a survey of the 20th and 21st century history of the ways in which the mission of the Shrine of Our Lady of Good Help was carried out, there are four definitive times the contemplative aspect of the mission was emphasized: (1) The Bay Settlement Sisters aspirancy and pre-novitiate high school; (2) The arrival of the Community of Our Lady; (3) The establishment of a House of Prayer; (4) The arrival of the Discalced Carmelite sisters.

In 1956, a dormitory was built on the shrine's grounds to house the growing number of vocations of a local religious community, the Sisters of St. Francis of the Holy Cross, known in common parlance as the Bay Settlement Sisters. It was the Bay Settlement Sisters who in 1902 accepted the two remaining tertiary Sisters

---

1   Dominica, 39.

2   I use the term Shrine of Our Lady of Good Help as it has come to be known today; back then the property was referred to as the Chapel of Our Lady of Good Help.

of Saint Francis.[3] Although the Bay Settlement Sisters are an active community of sisters who ran the school Adele started, the establishment of the aspirancy and pre-novitiate high school should be considered part of the contemplative mission. What better place to form future religious sisters for an active mission in the Church than at a place where Mary revealed a mission of prayer! In the high school pre-novitiate and formation program the sisters would be formed in the spiritual tradition of the Church and would have the potential to foster greater devotion to Mary. By being at the shrine, the sisters were preparing themselves to become the "Adele" of their time; first through prayer and reception of the sacraments and secondly by being sent out as teachers and missionaries.

In 1968 and 1969, the shrine welcomed a newly formed community of Benedictine monks, the Community of Our Lady. When the main Benedictine community in Cedarburg dissolved because of the monks' age, three younger members of the community requested permission to continue living the lifestyle.[4] Although the monks primarily sought to live the contemplative life, they also saw fit to provide devotions and sacramental care for the pilgrims who visited. The monks additionally chanted the Divine Office daily at the shrine and heard confessions Monday through Friday.[5] In response to Adele's contemplative mission, the monks mirrored that calling by providing the sacraments for those who sought the Eucharist and Penance. As a result, people were being prepared to become witnesses of Christ's love to the world. Additionally, the monks sought to live a contemplative life, to pray and meditate on scripture; arguably, they imitated Our Lady, for whom their community was named, by sitting quietly, reflecting on everything in their heart. Those who encountered the monks' contemplative life during their visit to the shrine encountered a unique calling in the church. One cannot help but be inspired by the life of those who dedicate themselves to prayer and contemplation. In encountering the Community of Our Lady, pilgrims received the opportunity to encounter Christ and Our Lady through their ministry.

---

3   Dominica, 39.

4   Sue Kaufman, "Robinsonville's Three Benedictine Monks Merge Contemplation, Restoration Work," *Green Bay Register,* Nov 29, 1968, 16.

5   Kaufman, 16.

The ministry of the Community of Our Lady lasted only one year at the shrine before the group settled in Oshkosh, where its ministry continues today. In 1973-74, the shrine became home to the Midwest Capuchins' House of Prayer, which "emphasized the apostolate of prayer."[6] The members of the Midwest Capuchins requested "opportunities to deepen their prayer life [... in order to] engage in more intensive prayer, contemplation and penance for the welfare of the Church and the Order."[7] This newly founded group sought to bring a place of prayer into the world, facilitated through the property at the shrine. The Midwest Capuchin's House of Prayer, like the Community of Our Lady, remained only one year, but in 1981-1988, the Bay Settlement Sisters, who throughout the turbulent years maintained their role of service to the shrine, began another house of prayer in order to be "an apostolate of radical witness to the importance of prayer."[8] The establishments of the houses of prayer recognize the importance of the spiritual growth for society and afforded that opportunity to those who made pilgrimages to the shrine. Since 1859, people had come to the chapel and the site of the apparition to pray for healings and special intentions. It had already been a house of prayer since the beginning, but through the ministry of the Capuchins and the Bay Settlement Sisters, this mission of prayer rose to the forefront. Just as Adele was instructed to make intercession for the world, so, too, are we invited to do likewise. The shrine provides the opportunity to grow closer to the Lord in prayer through the intercession of Our Lady.

In 1992, upon the invitation of then-Bishop Adam Maida and renewed by Bishop Robert Banks, the continual presence of intercessors for the salvation of the world became present on the shrine property until 2002, when the Discalced Carmelite Sisters took up residence there. In his homily establishing the enclosure of the Carmelite community, Bishop Banks reflected upon the meaning of the Carmelite vocation. He said, "They do penance for us and they pray for us. And we certainly need the prayers and penances. ...But, my friends, the ability to spend more time

---

6   Sept. 14, 1973, unknown newspaper article found in Diocesan archives.

7   Ibid.

8   Sister Sharron St. John, "Robinsonville Chapel Becomes House of Prayer Officially After Many Years," *The Spirit.*

in prayer is not the ultimate explanation of the cloister."[9] The reason one withdraws from the world to enter a cloister is out of love for Jesus. Citing the example of St. Therese of Lisieux, Banks said, "[I]t was love alone that enabled the Church to act; without love, nothing would happen."[10] The presence of the Carmelite Sisters help us to realize the importance of Mary's central message contained within the apparition's contemplative mission – to pray for the conversion of sinners. They take on penances for the salvation of the world out of love for Jesus. Their desire to serve Jesus and the Church is out of love for souls. The sisters' presence at the shrine allowed for the continuation of the sacraments for the pilgrims who were seeking Mary's intercession.

The contemplative mission entrusted to Adele is best seen lived in the twentieth century by the continual presence of "prayers" – monks and religious sisters. Their dedication and love for the Lord had the ability to inspire those who came to the shrine to a greater love and devotion for the Lord. The presence of the Community of Our Lady, the Midwest Capuchins, the Bay Settlement Sisters and the Discalced Carmelites provided a place of prayer and meditation to unite oneself to the Lord in prayer under Our Lady's intercession. As religious priests, brothers, and sisters, the religious who served the shrine throughout the years prayed for the Universal Church through the celebration of the Liturgy of the Hours, or Divine Office. The Liturgy of the Hours – the prayer of the Church – is undertaken for the whole people of God. Those who pray it

> bring growth to God's people in a hidden but fruitful apostolate, for the work of the apostolate is directed to this end, that all who are made children of God by faith and baptism should come together to praise God in the midst of this Church, to take part in the sacrifice, and to eat the Lord's Supper.[11]

Mary's wish for Adele to pray for the conversion of sinners is

---

9   Bishop Robert Banks, "The great, overwhelming vocation of love," *The Compass*, June 5. 1992, 3.

10   Ibid.

11   General Instruction of the Liturgy of the Hours, 18.

realized each time the religious pray the Divine Office, for they all desire to be united to the Lord. Additionally, in the recitation of the rosary, we pray for our own conversion and the conversion of others when we ask Mary to "pray for us sinners, now and at the hour of our death." The recitation of the Liturgy of the Hours and countless rosaries throughout the years by the religious and lay faithful at the shrine have facilitated their own conversion and that of the whole world while at the same time honoring Our Lady's request.

The Active Mission

Adele's active mission of catechesis and sacramental preparation was continued throughout the years in different ways, mainly through the ministry of the Bay Settlement Sisters. Following Adele's death, the Bay Settlement Sisters took on the remaining two tertiary sisters and were entrusted the school Adele had begun. In later years a home for crippled children was established on the property. Lastly, the sisters' continued presence, providing hospitality to pilgrims, exemplified Adele's mission being carried out in the 20th century.

Adele's initial mission to teach the children was brought to fulfillment through the establishment of a school. As such, after Adele's death the school had the potential to continue its founder's mission. In 1902, through the intervention of the Diocese of Green Bay and Bishop Sebastian Messmer, the mission begun by Adele was entrusted to the Bay Settlement Sisters under the direction of Sister Pauline.[12] In 1929, 44 years following the school's foundation, the Diocese of Green Bay chose to close the school in favor of supporting Guardian Angel Boarding School in Oneida.[13] As a result, the diocese entered into a period of discernment about the future mission of the property.

In 1933 Bishop Rhode announced the establishment of a crippled children's home. In a letter dated September 5, 1933 to the pastors and faithful of the Diocese of Green Bay asking for donations, Rhode acknowledged, "The one institution that we, up to the present, have not as yet and, whose need, is at

---

12   Sr. Paulette Hupfauf, "Bay Settlement Sisters Succeeded Adele", *The Compass*, May 22, 1992, 8A.

13   Sister M. Zita, "Origin and History of the Crippled Children" *At The Chapel*, July 1951, 2.

times sorely felt, is a home or an asylum for crippled children."[14] The home served those who were both mentally and physically handicapped, and students there would receive a diocesan eighth grade diploma. Part of the curriculum included daily religious instruction. Fr. Milo Smits, O.Praem, chaplain to the chapel and the home's superintendent, always had "the spiritual and temporal welfare of the children and Sisters" as his primary concern.[15] The home did not restrict itself to accepting Catholics, but Sister Zita's report indicates there were "five converts among the children. Of the thirteen that expect to return next September, twelve are Catholics. The other one greatly desires to become a Catholic. Her parents do not object."[16] The home provided children the care they needed. While most of society rejected them, the sisters provided them with care, attention, and both a secular and religious education. When others were unwilling to care for these children, the sisters gathered them together to teach them what they needed to know for salvation, just as Adele had done many years earlier. The home closed in 1953 because the need was no longer present, as other facilities were becoming more available. In addition, the upkeep and "changes in methods of care" prompted the decision of the diocese's decision.[17] The home's closure marked another chapter in the shrine's long history as a way in which Adele's mission continued after her death. The sisters' care and work for the conversion of souls was evident in the home's 20-year history.

The Bay Settlement Sisters remained active at the shrine from 1902 until the arrival of the Discalced Carmelite Sisters. Through teaching at the school, caring for disabled children, and showing hospitality to visitors during the years of transition, the sisters' goal was to engage in the shrine's active mission, fostering devotion and prayer to Our Lord through the intercession of His Mother Mary.

The Mission Today
In 2002, the Discalced Carmelite Sisters relocated to their

---

14   Paul P. Rhode, Letter to the Diocese, as found in the Diocesan archives, September 5, 1933.

15   Zita, 10.

16   Zita, 11.

17   "Robinsonville Home Closing", 7/2/1953. (Newspaper unknown, found in the Diocesan Archives).

new convent in Denmark, WI. During that time the shrine was served by retired priests of the Diocese of Green Bay. Prior to December 8, 2010, the shrine was a quiet and humble chapel, welcoming the occasional visitor, but it especially welcomed the regular devotees who had come to the property to pray for years. Once the apparitions received Church approval, the shrine was catapulted into the national and international sphere and began attracting visitors from all across the United States and around the world. Busloads of pilgrims came to petition the Blessed Mother in their time of need. Others have made the journey on foot whether it is a ten-mile walk or a 100+ mile journey.[18] Devotion to Our Lady at this shrine has increased exponentially.

Recognizing the need for sacramental care for the hundreds of pilgrims who come each day, Bishop David Ricken of the Diocese of Green Bay invited the Fathers of Mercy, based out of Kentucky, to establish a ministry at the shrine. They celebrate Mass and hear confessions on a daily basis. Additionally, the Fathers of Mercy have a specific charism for preaching, which is fitting to admonish and instruct the sinner. Adele was told to receive the Eucharist and to make a general confession. The Fathers' ministry helps to make that mandate possible for all the pilgrims who come so that after they leave the sacred ground, they too can go out to all the world and witness their Catholic faith to those around them.

In this third millennium, the era of the new evangelization, a time marked by atheism and relativism, Our Lady's mission of prayer, conversion, and catechesis strikes a chord within the human condition. The encounter each pilgrim has at the shrine, whether with Jesus reserved in the Blessed Sacrament, through reception of Holy Communion, or through the absolution of their sins; or whether it is a quiet, peaceful and abiding presence felt at the site of the apparition; the pilgrim must leave a different person – transformed by grace and the power of Mary's intercession. Upon departure, the pilgrim leaves the quiet sanctuary of Our Lady of Good Help to return to the world and light it ablaze. The shrine's mission today is to call us to live the simple message by our actions, in what we say and do. Joining

---

18   C.f. Edward Looney, "Walking pilgrimages: A tradition renewed at shrine," *The Compass*, August 11, 2011. It can be accessed online at: http://thecompassnews.org/news/local/2464-walking-pilgrimages-a-tradition-renewed-at-shrine.html

themselves to Adele's witness, pilgrims today can be inspired by the simplicity of a humble Belgian immigrant who was granted an extraordinary vision of Heaven. May the message of Our Lady, the Queen of Heaven, resound throughout our country and world, as we undertake the mission of the new evangelization through prayer, conversion, and catechesis.

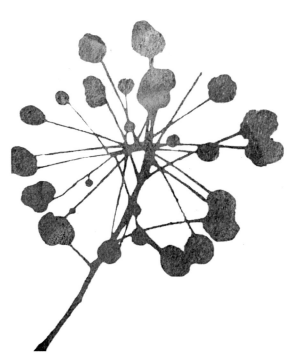

PART II:
UNDERSTANDING CHAMPION
<u>THEN AND NOW</u>

The message and mission entrusted to Adele in 1859 was of a personal nature which led her to teach young Belgian children. In effect, this apparition helped Adele discover her vocation in life. As already argued earlier in this book, this personal mission of prayer and apostolate should not be restricted to Adele alone but is meant for all those who learn of Mary's mission for Adele. The original message and mission had a specific purpose at that time, given the Belgian immigrants' laxity of spiritual practice. Mary's apparition served a particular purpose at that time. Today, the mission is really no different but is meant for a different time period. Since 1859, the shrine was a low-key apparition site attracting local people over the years. With the recent approval granted to Adele's visions, her message and mission are renewed in the modern era. People who had never heard of Adele, the shrine, or Champion have since begun to make pilgrimages to this holy site. Adele's message and mission can be best understood given the apparition's historical context, both then and now, as the message is always relevant.

CHAPTER 7:
CHAMPION THEN:
THE BALTIMORE COUNCILS

Throughout history, apparitions have served the purpose of religious renewal. They remind people of God's presence in the world and His Mother's desire that all may be saved and one day partake of the heavenly banquet. Her messages call sinners to repent and to draw closer to her Son through the sacraments and prayer. The Mariophany at Guadalupe occurred during a time of intensified human sacrifices; Mary appeared in a way that the Aztecs understood and accepted. Similarly, the 1858 manifestations of the Immaculate Conception at Lourdes affirmed the 1854 dogmatic declaration that Mary was conceived without original sin. This definition was important at the time, as secular forces were denying the reality of sin.

Besides the spiritual crisis plaguing the Belgian immigrant community, Adele's apparition affirms the First Plenary Council and complements the two later Baltimore Councils. Smaller councils led up to the plenary councils, which published decrees on behalf of the Church in America. The first provincial council in 1829 emphasized the importance of Catholic schools teaching young people the principles of faith and morality. The First Plenary Council of Baltimore (1852) emphasized the duty of catechesis by the clergy and the establishment of parochial schools.[1] Furthermore, the 1866 Plenary Council developed the necessity of catechetical sessions for those who attend public schools, especially those preparing for the sacraments.[2] The Third (and last) Plenary Council of Baltimore (1884) again stressed the need for Catholic schools and promulgated a Catechism of Christian Doctrine, which many have come to know as the *Baltimore Catechism*. The Councils that convened at Baltimore served as an aid not only to the [Arch]dioceses in the United States, but also to Adele as the Church continually, though

---

1   Peter Guilday, *A History of the Councils of Baltimore, 1791-1884* (New York: Macmillan, 1932), 179.

2   Guilday, 211.

indirectly, confirmed the work she was undertaking by showing her work was in cooperation with the bishops and priests.

The 1859 apparition to Adele, preceding the final two Plenary Councils of Baltimore, illustrates how Mary's revelation to Adele was aligned with the mind of the Church. Years before the conception of catechetical instruction for public school students, Adele was already teaching children of all backgrounds from her experience as a religious – by her simple love of the faith and with her personalized mission from the Mother of God. This mission can be derived from Adele's mission to teach the children the Catholic faith, namely, their catechism, how to make the Sign of the Cross, and how to approach the sacraments.

The Third Plenary Council later promulgated a new catechism. As the Church continued to evolve in its understanding of catechesis, it had become clear that it was indirectly affirming Mary's directives. The Church had realized the need for catechesis a few decades following the apparition to Adele. The simple work that Adele had first begun at Our Lady's command became systematized by the Church hierarchy for all the dioceses and archdioceses throughout the United States. Our Lady's message and mission was necessary not only for Adele but for the entire country. Seeing Champion in light of the Baltimore Councils helps to understand the apparition's purpose in the 19th century.

CHAPTER 8

CHAMPION NOW:
THE NEW EVANGELIZATION

On December 8, 2010, Bishop Ricken decreed that the apparitions and locutions to Adele were worthy of belief.[1] Why was Our Lady's message taking center-stage then, after 150+ years of having a quiet, humble following? At Champion, the sun did not spin (as happened at Fatima) and no miraculous spring was found (as at Lourdes). The most miraculous event occurred twelve years after the apparition – the sparing of the property and those gathered at the shrine on the night of the Peshtigo Fire. Mary's appearance to Adele was not extravagant but rather simple; it was to encourage Adele in her faith and to respond to a call for catechesis.

Pope Paul VI first wrote about the need for a new evangelization in *Evangelii Nuntiandi*, and Pope John Paul II wrote about it extensively throughout his papacy. In their writings, both popes described society as being marked by defiance to Church authority, a decline in the sacramental life of the Church (especially in Mass attendance and Sacrament of Penance), a breakdown in the family, secularization, and atheism.[2] Noticing these problems, John Paul wrote his first encyclical, *Redemptor Hominis*, calling mankind to rediscover its Redeemer. His Holiness continued to develop his vision of the new evangelization over the course of his pontificate. The hallmark of John Paul's program for the new evangelization was straightforward – man needed to encounter the Lord in both

---

1   C.f. Most Reverend David L. Ricken, "Decree on the Authenticity of the Apparitions of 1859 at the Shrine of Our Lady of Good Help", Diocese of Green Bay, http://www.gbdioc.org/images/stories/Evangelization_Worship/Shrine/Documents/Shrine-of-Our-Lady-of-Good-Help.pdf (accessed April 12, 2011).

2   Pope Paul VI, *Evangelii Nuntiandi* (Washington DC: United States Catholic Conference, 8 Dec 1975).
Pope John Paul II. *Ecclesia in America* (Washington DC: United States Catholic Conference, 22 Jan. 1999).
Pope John Paul II, *Novo Millenio Ineunte*, (Boston: Pauline Books & Media, 6 Jan 2001).

Word and Sacrament. By drawing near to Scripture, the Mass, and the Sacrament of Penance, one is given the necessary graces to persevere in the spiritual and moral life.

Under Pope Benedict XVI the Church continued to call the faithful to evangelization. In September 2010, Benedict initiated the Pontifical Council for Promoting the New Evangelization through his *motu proprio, Ubicumque et Semper.* Benedict realized that the need for catechesis and evangelization was still prevalent, and like his predecessors, he continued to make evangelization a priority. The Pontifical Council encouraged the use of the Catechism of the Catholic Church and explored new ways of evangelizing in the third millennium.[3] In the Year of Faith, commemorating the fiftieth anniversary of the Second Vatican Council, Benedict convened a special synod on the new evangelization.

The apparitions' approval allowed for Our Lady's message and story to resurface in an era marked with the same trends as of old – an era where Catholics have been raised in their faith but do not necessarily practice or even understand its basic tenets. Adele's message and mission were relevant in their day with the Baltimore Councils and remain relevant today, cooperating with the movement and direction of the Church under the Holy Father, because they provide a blueprint for catechesis and evangelization. By knowing the apparition's historical context, one is then able to understand the apparition's further implications in the life of the Church by proposing a way of life for all believers.

The new evangelization does not necessarily call us to have better materials or to reach out in new and different ways. Rather, it focuses on returning to the source of all life – the same wellspring which Adele drew from – the Sacraments of Eucharist and Penance coupled with personal prayer. Catechists first need to be formed in the spiritual life so that they truly believe what they confess before being able to relay the faith to others. Re-echoing Paul VI, they must first be witnesses of the Christian life before they can be teachers.

The story of Adele, her shrine, and the apparitions have

---

3   Pope Benedict XVI, *"Ubicumque Et Semper,"* Vatican: the Holy See, http://www.vatican. va/holy_father/benedict_xvi/apost_letters/documents/hf_ben-xvi_apl_20100921_ ubicumque-et-semper_en.html (Accessed April 5, 2011).

the potential to transform the lives of many as they encounter Jesus Christ in the simplicity of this third-order laywoman. As a Church, we can be inspired by the fervor of the saints who were great preachers and evangelizers.[4] Although Adele has not been beatified, her life was marked by extraordinary events that are able to inspire us today. Like Adele, who learned from the Queen of Heaven, the Mother of all catechists, the Blessed Mother asks us to learn our faith before relaying it to others.

The history of the Americas and the evangelization that has occurred has been profoundly influenced by a Marian dimension, beginning with Christopher Columbus' Marian piety and culminating with Mary's concern for sinners at Guadalupe and Champion. The messages given to Guadalupe visionary Juan Diego and Adele are not archaic messages of yesteryear but are still relevant even today. In a time of immense spiritual need, the Queen of Heaven appeared to a simple Belgian immigrant in the middle of a wooded settlement, entrusting to her a specific mission of prayer and service.

This mission for evangelization provides a basis for catechesis. Looking to Adele, we return to the fundamentals of the faith. The mission points individuals toward conversion as they encounter the Lord through the Blessed Virgin's motherly guidance and intercession. With the approval of the Champion apparition, the message is no longer limited to the Diocese of Green Bay or even the United States but is a message for the entire world. The Queen of Heaven guides us to a way of life which is crucial in this age of the new evangelization. She provided a blueprint for evangelization for her people, first in Guadalupe and then in Champion. Today these methods are more important than ever. May the blueprint entrusted to those visionaries and the Church at large be a call to which God's holy people always respond. Our Lady, Queen of Heaven and of Good Help, pray for us as we pray and work for the conversion of sinners in our day and age. May your message be heard by the entire world today as it was 150+ years ago by Adele's unfailing trust and belief in those miraculous events.

---

4   EN, 80.

CHAPTER 9:
CONTEMPORARY APPLICATION OF MESSAGE AND MISSION

Adele's message and mission to pray for the conversion of sinners and catechize young people has practical applications for today. Our culture is saturated in a lifestyle of sin, whether known or unbeknown to the average person. Society is plagued by atheism, secularism, and relativism. It is marked by promiscuous sexual lifestyles, prostitution, homosexuality, and the legalization of abortion. Society's moral conscience and compass has gone awry.

Anybody who drives along an interstate for any given amount of time is bound to see billboards and business along the highway. Some of these billboards advertise "adult superstores" or "adult video stores." These signs and businesses are reminiscent of our sexually perverse culture and the dehumanization of the dignity of man and woman. A good practice when driving by these stores would be to pray for the conversion of those who work in the pornography industry, that they will experience a conversion of heart. Or better yet, that these stores will close not because pornography would one day become illegal, but because people stop frequenting these stores because they no longer desire to purchase their product.

The central message of most Marian apparitions is to pray for the conversion of sinners. Mary herself, as the Queen of Heaven told Adele that she prays for the conversion of sinners. Citing Adele's example, prayer alone is not enough; one must also work for the conversion of sinners. Praying for the conversion of the pornography industry and its consumers is not enough. It is necessary to instruct others about the dignity of the human person and why sexual sins are wrong. People need to be instructed as to why the sexual act should be done only within the context of marriage, where it finds its proper expression and fulfillment, and how sex should not be meant for entertainment but rather reserved for procreation and union between man and woman. Pornography dehumanizes the person participating in the act and those who view it, and it also degrades the sexual act itself by diminishing its purpose within marriage. It is not enough for a person to be told not to commit sins against chastity; he or she must be told why these things are wrong. Catechesis on topics of sexuality, by using John Paul II's Theology of the Body as an example, can help to facilitate the conversion that many have prayed for over the years. It is only through instruction that "sinners" are able to realize the error of their ways and thereby confront and correct their behavior.

This idea perhaps is best seen in an anecdotal story. A priest once preached on how he consistently prayed for the poor and homeless, that God would help them find shelter and provide for their needs. One day after walking by a homeless person, he realized that he had to do something to help them. He realized that he had to cooperate with his own prayers, and that God could use him to answer his own prayer by helping the poor and homeless himself. In the example of the pornography industry, sometimes people at work or with friends casually talk about immoral sexual acts, whether they have practiced it themselves or even jokingly talking about it. These are opportunities where a person with a well formed conscience and an understanding of theology could catechize the individuals about the dignity of the human person and the sacredness of the sexual act.

In contemporary society, Adele's Mariophany helps us to understand that sometimes we are the answer to our own prayers. Adele's prayer for the conversion of sinners was coupled with her participation in her active mission of catechesis. If we desire to live Our Lady's message, the same may be true for us. Our Lady has asked us to pray and now she asks us to do just a little more by the witness of our lives.

PART III:

UNDERSTANDING CHAMPION IN LIGHT OF APPROVED MARIAN APPARITIONS

Mary has appeared in many locations throughout history, but only a few of those apparitions have ever been validated or approved by the Church. Champion joins an elite group of apparitions including Guadalupe, Lourdes, and Fatima, among others. Why does Mary appear? She appears at particular moments in history to guide God's people back to Him. In her apparitions, she never brings the focus on herself, but always directs us to the sacraments – to the Eucharist and Penance. In Guadalupe, Lourdes, Fatima, and Beauraing, Mary desired that a church be built – a place where Mass would be offered and people could come and pray. Mary desires to put a wayward people back in a right relationship with their Heavenly Father. As a loving mother, Mary comes to guide us on our way toward salvation.

In reading about any Mariophany, one will notice many similarities, especially Mary's desire for the salvation of souls. The conversion of sinners seems to be a typical theme for most messages. In reading the story of Juan Diego one can find many similarities between Adele Brise and Juan Diego regarding their lives, message, and mission each received. In Part III, Champion will be analyzed in light of other approved apparitions. To a certain degree, all Mariophanies are related, and one can notice a progression in the message, as if a torch has been passed on to Mary's next revelation. Mary's message and mission to Juan Diego is a similarly lived message and mission in Champion by Adele. The apparitions of Champion and Lourdes could be viewed as bookends to each other. Fatima could be viewed as an intensification of the Champion message and mission. Lastly, Our Lady's apparition to a Belgian immigrant in 1859 is mirrored by another Mariophany to five Belgian children in Beauraing, Belgium. These apparitions should not be seen in isolation from one another but in complete complementarity. Private Marian revelation should be viewed as a collective whole.

By understanding the shrine in life, name, message and mission, we can better understand what the Mariophany means in light of other approved revelations of the Catholic Church.

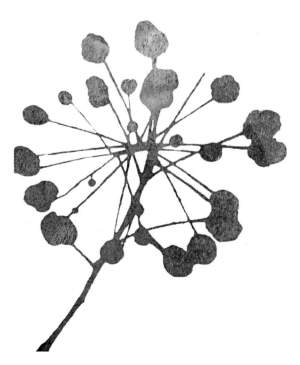

CHAPTER 10:
THE PARALLELS OF GUADALUPE AND CHAMPION

The year was 1519; Spanish conquistadors led by Hernando Cortes just arrived in the New World to explore and colonize New Spain.[1] Upon landing they discovered the Aztec civilization, the mode of governance of the colonies and the religion of the Aztec people—the worship of the gods and goddesses: sun, rain, wind, and fire.[2] Their worship extended to the point of offering sacrifices to appease the gods or to prevent future misfortune. Unlike the biblical notion of offering animals in sacrifice, "they felt driven to supply this divinity [the sun] with a regular 'nourishment' of human blood," typically the blood of slaves or prisoners of war.[3] Christian missionaries arrived in an attempt to Christianize the colonies but for the most part were unsuccessful. A spiritual crisis was emerging.

Over 300 years later in the United States of America a wave of immigrants from Europe arrived.[4] Local churches became overwhelmed with the pastoral need to address the growing immigrant church throughout the country causing the rise of national churches.[5] Like the rest of the United States, Northeastern Wisconsin saw its share of immigrants especially

---

1   The Handbook of Guadalupe provides two chapters on the Evangelization of the New World; see: Bro. Francis Mary, FFI, "Catholic Spain in the Evengelization of the New World" in *A Handbook on Guadalupe* (New Bedford: Academy of the Immaculate, 1997), 19-23. And: Diana Cary, "Cortes and the Valiant "Little Ladies" in *A Handbook on Guadalupe*, 35-40.

2   Francis Johnston, *The Wonders of Guadalupe* (Rockford: TAN Books and Publishers, 1981), 12.

3   Johnston, 12-13.

4   Marcus Hansen provides a brief commentary on the language problems for immigrants in his work *The Immigrant in American History*. See: Marcus Hansen, *The Immigrant in American History* (Cambridge: Harvard University Press, 1942), 146-7. Another work addressing the issue of immigration is: John F. Kennedy, *A Nation of Immigrants* (New York: Harper and Row, 1964), 17-63.

5   Jay Dolan provides a good commentary on the rise of national churches. C.f. Jay Dolan, *In Search of An American Catholicism* (New York: Oxford University Press, 2002), 60-61; 133-134.

those of Belgian descent. As the Belgians settled in the Door Peninsula, in 1853 missionary Crosier Father Edward Daems provided for their sacramental care, however, after his transfer by the diocese to another post, it would be three years until his return.[6] In the interim, Rev. John Perrodin made infrequent visits to the peninsula, and in a letter to a European pastor he wrote:

> For the spiritual account unfortunately there is much to lose for the Catholic emigrant...They end up by neglecting their duties of religion and live as unbelievers. The children are not instructed and grow up without knowing God.... Would there be any priests in Belgium zealous enough to accompany their flocks?[7]

Suffice to say, the faith of the Belgians suffered because they were without a spiritual father who would instruct them on a regular basis. A spiritual crisis was emerging.

Besides the evident spiritual crises both in Mexico in the 1500s and Northeastern Wisconsin in the 1850s, these two events share more in common. In time and space, both were places of intervention through a Mariophany to two visionaries – Juan Diego and Adele Brise. There are many similarities between Guadalupe and Champion, beginning with the implied message of evangelization and extending to the life and mission the visionaries undertook as a result of the apparition. This chapter will show the interconnectedness of the two apparitions in light of the visionaries' lives and visions and the content of their respective Mariophanies.

The Early Lives of Juan Diego and Adele Brise

The more contemporary apparitions of the Blessed Virgin Mary, of which arguably the most popular are Lourdes and Fatima, share a similarity – the visionaries or seers were young children or adolescents born into poor peasant or lower class families. In Guadalupe something entirely different is found. While it is true Juan Diego was poor and merely educated to

---

6   Dominica, 1-2.

7   Dominica, 3.

the extent of preparation for the workforce, [8] Our Lady appeared to someone who was not a child, but was "already in the prime of life."[9] Similarly, Adele, who came from a poor immigrant working family and received a very meager education in Belgium,[10] received her apparition at the age of 28. Prior to their respective Mariophanies, both were considered to be devout, pious persons.[11] The Blessed Virgin chose Juan Diego and Adele to receive a message along with a specific mission. Mary did not choose children for the task of catechesis or to relay her message to the world; instead, she chose poor and unlearned instruments who would be capable of transmitting the faith through teaching others by the witness of their lives.

The Message

Juan Diego and Adele's apparitions came at a particular junction in their lives in which their vocational calling was made clearer vis-à-vis the content of the message and the mission they received. The days in which both saw the Blessed Virgin and received their message were marked by the same occurrence – they were on the way to and/or[12] from Mass. Juan Diego and Adele both had to walk long distances from their homes to arrive at the church; for Juan Diego it was a nine-mile journey,[13] and Adele had to make an eleven-mile trek.[14] The key phrases contained within Juan's dialogue with the Virgin in relation to the Champion apparition are as follows: [15]

---

8   Dr. Charles Wahlig, "Juan Diego: Ambassador of Heaven" in *A Handbook on Guadalupe* (New Bedford: Academy of the Immaculate, 1997), 44. Wahlig provides a commentary on the contemporary discussion pertaining to Juan Diego's poverty. The class to which Juan Diego belonged was a property-owning class either from inheritance, working, or both. The poverty of Juan Diego in historical study concludes he undertook it voluntarily.

9   Fr. Christopher Rengers, OFM Cap, "Mother of the Americas" in *A Handbook on Guadalupe*, 3.

10   Dominica, 5.

11   For the testimony regarding Adele's virtue see Dominica, 6. For testimony regarding Juan Diego see Johnston, 24-5; Wahlig, 44.

12   The second and third apparitions received by Adele occurred on Sunday October 9, 1859, first on the way to the church and then upon her return from Mass. It was during the third apparition Our Lady spoke to Adele. During the first apparition, Our Lady did not relay a message then either.

13   Wahlig, 46; Johnston, 25.

14   Dominica, 8.

15   The content of the dialogue with Juan Diego is taken from the *Nican Mopohua* as

In the first apparition:

1. Our Lady asked Juan where he was going.

2. Mary identifies herself as the ever Virgin Holy Mary, Mother of the God of truth.

3. Juan Diego was told that he would be the means by which Mary's compassionate and merciful objective would be achieved.

4. Mary acknowledged her gratitude and promised to help him as she sent him forth on his mission.

Second apparition:

5. Juan Diego begged Our Lady to send one of the nobles who were held in high esteem and respected to convey her message to the bishop.

The dialogue between Juan Diego and Our Lady represents a similar dialogue between Adele and the Queen of Heaven. In her identification at Tepeyac as the Holy Virgin Mary, Mother of the God of truth, Mary places her identity as Mother of the true God in contrast to the Aztec gods whom the Indians were worshipping. Even though Juan Diego had already been converted, Mary's name would be important in relaying her identity in his work of evangelization. Mary places herself in a distinct way from the Aztec goddess Tonantzin[16] and appears over the site of where a temple once stood to this pagan goddess.[17] As the Mother of the true God, Mary replaces Tonantzin and beckons the Indians to the true God – Jesus Christ. In Champion, Mary identified herself as "the Queen of Heaven who prays for the conversion of sinners."[18] It would appear the connection that both identifications shared was Our Lady's desire for the salvation of souls. She desired the conversion of the Aztecs, and she desired the return of the

found in *A Handbook on Guadalupe*, 193-204.

16   Johnston, 13.

17   Johnston, 13.

18   Dominica, 8.

Belgians who had become lax in the practice of their Catholic faith. In both ways, Mary reveals the *sitz im leben*[19](oppressed Aztec culture – alienated, impoverished French Belgian Door County) – the need for conversion to the Catholic faith.

Our Lady asked Juan Diego where he was going. He was headed to the church for Mass and instruction on the feast of the Immaculate Conception (then observed on December 9). For Adele, she had seen Mary on her way to Mass and spoke with her on the way back. The Queen of Heaven commended Adele for her reception of Holy Communion but exhorted her to do more – to pray for the conversion of sinners through the offering of future Holy Communions and to make a general confession.

The importance of Adele's preparation for her mission also reflects the fact that Juan Diego could only fulfill Mary's wishes by going to the bishop and requesting that a sanctuary be built in her honor. In the same way, Adele was the instrument through which Our Lady's objective of catechesis and conversion would be brought about. Juan Diego and Adele both felt unqualified for the mission. Juan Diego requested that Mary send another noble person to speak to the bishop, while Adele asked Our Lady, "But how shall I teach them who know so little myself?"[20] Adele did not believe herself to be worthy of the mission because she was a poor, uneducated immigrant who was blind in one eye. Nevertheless, Our Lady found her to be qualified because she could teach from her own knowledge of faith and from her relationship with the Lord. Furthermore, the Mariophany she received would become the conduit of teaching as she relayed the marvelous event to those she met.

Lastly, both were sent off with a blessing and promised help from Mary. Juan Diego was told that even in "the fatigue, the work and trouble that my mission will cause you" he would be rewarded.[21] Juan Diego would face the rejection of the bishop after his first visit and suffer other afflictions, but in the end he would be rewarded as proven with the *tilma* and the widespread belief that followed. Adele was told, "Go and fear nothing, I will help you."[22] Like Juan Diego, Adele suffered adversity, rejection

---

19   German theological term in biblical criticism meaning "setting in life."

20   Dominica, 9.

21   Handbook, 196

22   Dominica, 9.

by some in the community, the loss of Belgians to the Old Catholic heresy,[23] and temporary ecclesiastical problems because of misunderstandings that reached the bishop.[24] But through it all, Adele received the heavenly guidance and intercession of Mary. Even amidst their lowliness and unworthiness to undertake their missions on behalf of Heaven, Juan Diego and Adele went forward from their apparitions sent as missionaries to those they encountered – spreading the gospel of Jesus Christ and their private encounter with Mary.

Mission

The Franciscan Renewal Center in Scottsdale, Arizona adorns an outdoor shrine and altar to Our Lady of Guadalupe. In addition to a large image of *La Virgen*, a mural of Juan Diego gathering people and sharing the story of the apparition as he

---

23 In the Door Peninsula, Joseph Rene Vilatte, an Old Catholic priest, sought to gain converts to his heretical sect. C.f. Dominica, 24-26.

24 At times in the life of Sr. Adele's ministry, false rumors had spread to the bishop which caused him to place a temporary interdict on the chapel and closing the school. After conversing with Adele, admiring her zeal for the salvation of souls, he ordered the school and chapel to be reopened. Cf. Dominica, 21-22.

displays the *tilma* can be found. The image depicts Juan Diego as a missionary who traveled the surrounding area to share the story of the apparition and gain converts. The message of Guadalupe, accompanied by Juan Diego's mission, resulted in the massive conversion of the native people. Conversion accounts are numerous with claims of 9 million conversions, stories of priests performing 6,000 baptisms per day, and an account of how one priest baptized over one million people throughout his life.[25]

Juan Diego was a layman and a convert. At one time he was married, but his wife died prior to Mary's appearance.[26] Following the reception of Mary's message and the *tilma*, Juan Diego was placed "in charge of the new chapel, to which a room was added for his accommodation...[where he] devote[d] the rest of his life to the custody of the new shrine and to propagating the story and explaining the significance of the apparitions."[27] Helen Behrens commented that

> [h]e told [the Indians] the story of the apparitions and repeated the loving words of the Blessed Virgin over and over again, thousands of times, until all knew the story. When the Indians presented themselves to the missionaries, they had already been converted by Juan Diego.[28]

Juan Diego's mission was to inform the bishop of Mary's desire for a church to be built at the site of the apparition so that she could be the Mother of the Afflicted. However, his mission extended beyond that simple and specific mission. It entailed an even broader mission to share the message he had received so that others may acknowledge Jesus Christ as the true God. Through Our Lady and her apparition, the faith was entrusted to millions through her simple messenger, Juan Diego, first to the bishop but then to the rest of the New World.

When viewing the image of Juan Diego teaching with the

---

25   Johnston, 56-7.

26   Carl Anderson, *Our Lady of Guadalupe: Mother of the Civilization of Love* (New York: Doubleday, 2009), 5.

27   Johnston, 54-5.

28   Helen Behrens, quoted in Johnston, 55.

tilma, one cannot help but see the parallel between Juan Diego sharing the story of the *tilma* and Adele's mission of teaching the young people their catechism, how to make the Sign of the Cross, and how to approach the sacraments. Similarly, Adele could be pictured in the fields of the Door Peninsula or on the chapel property with children gathered around her, intently listening to her story of Mary's marvelous apparition. Adele's missionary zeal led her on a

> mission going from house to house and helping unsolicited to do whatever work there was to be done in the household – asking only in return that she be permitted to give instruction to the children. …. Rain, snow, or heat did not prevent her from accomplishing her work; neither did fatigue or ridicule have any effect upon her.[29]

Seven years after these missionary efforts in a fifty mile radius, Adele settled near the chapel built by her father and upon the instruction of Fr. Phillip Crud, who "advised her to encourage others to share her labors. … He urged her to appeal for funds, to build a Convent and school where the children could come to her for instruction."[30] By 1867 and 1868 the convent and school had been established, and Adele's lay tertiary group, the Sisters of Good Help (often referred to erroneously as the Sisters of Good Health), "was established, and recognized by the Bishop of the diocese as a regular auxiliary of the Church."[31] Fr. Crud's vision was realized, and Adele began a more centralized and localized means of catechesis for the young people in accord with her mission. While Adele did not convert a nation or millions, she worked diligently for the salvation of souls, one by one, in her missionary efforts.

Juan Diego and Adele were both lay people whom the Blessed Mother had entrusted with a specific mission. While Adele is often referred to as "Sister" Adele, the order of sisters she found were a lay tertiary group of Franciscans. In the 1850s, it would have been common to refer to tertiaries as "Sister," and

---

29   Dominica, 9-10.

30   Dominica, 11.

31   Dominica, 14.

there are records of Adele being called *Soeur* by the bishop[32] and others who knew her. Timothy Matovina cites the hagiography of *Huei tlmanhuicolitca* which "depicts Juan Diego as a model Franciscan lay brother."[33] If this is the case, vocationally, both visionaries lived the life of lay Franciscan brother- and sisterhood. The means in which they lived their vocations was through catechesis and as custodians of the respective chapels built to foster devotion to Mary. Secondly, in carrying out their mission, Juan Diego and Adele became the vehicles through which Mary's messages were conveyed. Juan Diego had a distinct instrument for catechesis – the *tilma*, while Adele had clear instructions what to teach the young children. Thirdly, both were involved in the sacramental preparation for those whom they catechized. Juan Diego presented to the missionaries the converts he had gained for baptism, while Adele presented the children to the local priest for examination and admittance to Holy Communion.[34] Fourthly, both worked in cooperation with their bishop; even when Adele found herself at odds with the local bishop, she obediently followed his directives. Lastly, Juan Diego and Adele faithfully lived their missions. Juan Diego sought out the bishop to have a church built, at which he served for the rest of his life. Adele faithfully taught the local children by walking around the settlement but also through the establishment of a school and a convent. Both died having lived a life worthy of the call and mission they had received.

Conclusion

Guadalupe and Champion share a number of parallels in their visionaries' respective lives and missions. Notably, both apparitions occurred in the Americas, making them American[35] apparitions, and both had a purpose within their given timeframe.

---

32   In a letter dated December 10, 1895 obtained from the Diocesan archives, Bishop Joseph Fox writes, "There is a place, however -- Robinsonville with Soeur Adele – where they could put the boy and the board would be very cheap." The letter was in response to a request for a boy to be accepted into an orphanage run by the diocese.

33   Timothy Matovina, "Theologies of Guadalupe: From the Spanish Colonial Era to Pope John Paul II" *Theological Studies* 70, 2009, 70. C.f. Anderson, 132. Anderson's treatment of Our Lady of Guadalupe includes a chapter on Juan Diego's vocation in which he provides a synopsis of the situation regarding the barring of Indians from Holy Orders. In 1539 the bishops permitted Indians to join minor orders.

34   Dominica, 10.

35   This term is used loosely in this context to refer to North, South and Central America.

Our Lady came at a pivotal point in the evangelization of the New World in 1531 and ushered in the conversion of millions. The missionaries' program was not working, so Our Lady came with her tool for evangelization, namely the *tilma*. Similarly, in 1859, when immigrants were falling away from the faith and not preparing their children for the sacraments, Our Lady instructed Adele to teach young people the basics of the Catholic faith.

Since the promulgation of Paul VI's encyclical *Evangelii Nuntiandi*, coupled with the pontificates of John Paul II and Benedict XVI, there has been a new emphasis on the new evangelization – how to make the gospel relevant in today's world. In the fall of 2012 a synod of bishops was convened in Rome to address the new evangelization. In the United States the USCCB Committee on Evangelization and Catechesis released a document entitled "Disciples Called to Witness," reflecting on methods of evangelization in America. The Church can look to Juan Diego and Adele, who were disciples called to witness in their respective times in history in order to facilitate the conversions. Their witness still inspires the Church today as it comes to a better understanding of catechesis. With the recent approval given to the Champion apparition, evangelization has begun to take a more visible place within the Catholic Church in America. With pilgrims visiting each day, praying at the site of the apparition, receiving Holy Communion and absolution, asking Mary to "pray for us sinners," and visiting Adele's grave, they too are being taught by Adele.

The legacies of Juan Diego and Adele continue to this very day, and their messages should be seen not in opposition but in tandem with each other. Their historical settings, lives, messages, and missions can assist the Church today in understanding how to respond to the current crisis of faith – a crisis of atheism and relativism. In a time when a new evangelization is needed and has been called for, these Marian apparitions can become guiding principles, allowing Mary to become the guiding star. May the new evangelization's efforts be guided by the Star of the New Evangelization, the Virgin Mother of the true God and the Queen of Heaven. May the Church, through her intercession and by the inspiration of St. Juan Diego and Sister Adele, gain converts to the Catholic faith in the way and manner these two visionaries did during their earthly sojourn.

CHAPTER 11:

BOOKEND APPARITIONS:
LOURDES AND CHAMPION

Following Bishop Ricken's approval of the Champion apparition, Fr. James Martin, SJ, author of the books *Between Heaven and Mirth, My Life with the Saints* and *The Jesuit Guide to (Almost) Everything: A Spirituality for Real Life*, wrote a reflection on the connections between Lourdes and Champion. With the permission of Fr. Martin and *America Magazine*, the article is reproduced below. Following his thoughts, I will also provide a brief commentary.

First Marian Apparition in US
Approved by Fr. James Martin, SJ[1]

The church has approved (as "worthy of belief") for the first time a Marian apparition in the United States, after a two-year investigation by the local bishop. Bishop David L. Ricken of Green Bay has approved the apparitions of the Blessed Virgin Mary as seen by Adele Brise in Champion, Wis., in 1859. Bishop Ricken stated in a letter: "I declare with moral certainty and in accord with the norms of the Church that the events, apparitions and locutions given to Adele Brise in October of 1859 do exhibit the substance of supernatural character, and I do hereby approve these apparitions as worthy of belief (although not obligatory) by the Christian faithful." The website for the Shrine of Our Lady of Good Help has the story of the apparitions and the life of Sister Adele.

There are several notable similarities to the more well known apparitions at Lourdes, France, to St. Bernadette Soubirous, besides simply the timing. (Lourdes: 1858; Champion: 1859). In both cases, the apparitions were to a woman who had struggled with physical infirmities (Bernadette suffered from asthma; Adele lost an eye in an accident); in both cases the woman was

---

1   This article originally appeared in America magazine's blog "In All Things" and was subsequently published by multiple Catholic newspapers, including the Green Bay Diocese's *The Compass*.

at the time outdoors, in the midst of carrying out taxing physical chores (Bernadette looking for firewood for her family; Adele Brise carrying wheat to a mill); in both cases the women were poor but pious Catholics; in both cases the woman was most likely seen as on the margins of society (Bernadette's indigent family was living in a converted jail cell; Adele was a part of a poor immigrant population) in both cases the local pastor asked for an identification from the vision (Bernadette's pastor, Abbe Peyramale asks; Brise's pastor asks as well); in both cases the identification given was concise (Lourdes: "I am the Immaculate Conception"; Champion: "I am the Queen of Heaven"); in both cases Mary asks for prayers for sinners; in both cases the visionary later became associated with a religious order (Bernadette enters the Sisters of Nevers; Adele a group of Third Order Franciscans); and in both cases a chapel is built on the spot of the apparitions, which alters the original appearance of the site (in Lourdes the Grotto is paved over and the course of the nearby Gave River is changed; in Champion, the trees in which the Virgin appeared are felled to make room for the chapel); and in both cases the chapels later receive many visitors and miracles become associated with pilgrimages to the shrine. (End of Martin article)

Fr. Martin provides a basic overview or synopsis of the connections between Champion and Lourdes that scratches the surface. Given the similarities he has pointed out, there is no need to do an in-depth analysis of Champion in light of Lourdes. There is, however, one more interesting similarity. Fr. Martin indicated that the identity of Our Lady at each apparition was concise. Given the timeline of the two apparitions, the names reveal to us an even greater similarity – they are bookends of Mary's life. In 1858, Mary identified herself as the Immaculate Conception, which acknowledged the Church's recently pronounced dogmatic declaration that Mary was preserved from the stain of original sin. The following year, Our Lady identified herself as the Queen of Heaven, marking Mary's eschatological role in Heaven. Thus, Mary revealed the beginning of her earthly life to Bernadette and the culmination of her exalted identity to Adele. Mary's identification as the Queen of Heaven who specifically prays for the conversion of sinners resonates with her request of Saint Bernadette to pray for sinners and to do penance. Mary's revelation in 1858 to St. Bernadette was needed in France and a year later the same message was echoed and received by Adele Brise in the United States of America.[2] Given the timeframe of the apparitions, within one year of each other, the apparitions share similar messages, and the visionaries shared similar life experiences. In both Lourdes and Champion, we discover the love Mary has for the world by giving a message to simple visionaries, and that love is continually experienced in the years following the apparitions to the present day.

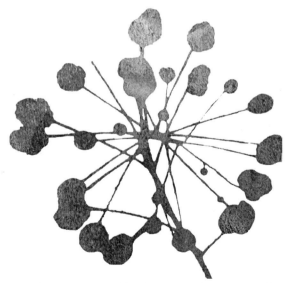

---

2   A few years following 1859, the Civil War would break out. Mary's message to Adele Brise seems to have historical implications for the United States. Mary revealed her desire for the conversion of sinners. She knew if people did not convert (in this case their opinions), there would be consequences, a civil war over several issues, including slavery.

CHAPTER 12:
EUCHARISTIC REPARATION
AND THE CONVERSION OF SINNERS:
FATIMA AND CHAMPION

In 1917, in the village of Fatima, Portugal, Mary, under the title of Our Lady of the Rosary, chose to manifest herself to three shepherd children – Lucia dos Santos and her cousins Jacinta and Francisco Marto. Prior to Mary's appearance to the children, they received three apparitions of an angel, who called himself the Angel of Peace. Between the angelic apparitions and those of Our Lady, a common theme emerges from the Fatima apparitions – prayer for the conversion of sinners, Eucharistic reparation, the rosary, and prayer for world peace. Given the message these children received, Fatima can be seen as an intensification of the Champion message. It is a further development of Mary's message and mission to Adele, in which we find a change in the language Our Lady used.

The Angelic Apparitions: Adoration and Reparation

In 1916 and 1917 the three shepherd children were taught specific prayers of adoration and reparation by the Angel of Peace. During the first angelic apparition, the children were taught the follow prayer: "My God, I believe, I adore, I hope and I love you. I ask pardon of you for those who do not believe, do not adore, do not hope and do not love you."[1] No prayer was taught during the second angelic apparition, but the angel encouraged them to pray and offer sacrifices "as an act of reparation for the sins by which [God] is offended and in supplication for the conversion of sinners. You will thus draw down peace upon your country."[2] In the third and final angelic apparition, the angel had in his possession a communion host and chalice for adoration, and he

---

1   The quotations and descriptions about the Fatima apparition come from Lucia's memoirs as quoted in: Mark Miravalle, "Marian Private Revelation: Nature, Evaluation, Message, in *Mariology: A Guide for Priests, Deacons, Seminarians and Consecrated Persons* (Goleta, CA: Queenship Publishing, 2007), 863.

2   Miravalle, 864.

taught the children the following prayer:

> Most Holy Trinity, Father, Son, and Holy Spirit, I adore you profoundly, and I offer you the most precious Body, Blood, Soul and Divinity of Jesus Christ, present in all the tabernacles of the world, in reparation for the outrages, sacrileges, and indifference with which he himself is offended. And, through the infinite merits of His most Sacred Heart, and the Immaculate Heart of Mary, I beg of you the conversion of poor sinners.[3]

Following the prayer, the angel then distributed the Eucharistic species to the children – the Host to Lucia and the Precious Blood to Jacinta and Francisco. Upon reception of Holy Communion the angel said, "Take and drink the Body and Blood of Jesus Christ, horribly outraged by ungrateful men! Make reparation for their crimes and console your God."[4] These three angelic apparitions' message was reparation for sin made through the personal offering of the Eucharist.

Fifty-seven years earlier in Champion, the same themes were present. At the core of the Champion apparition was the conversion of sinners through prayer and catechesis. Adele was instructed to offer her Holy Communion for the conversion of sinners. The instruction to the Fatima children to do likewise was intensified by the request to also make an offering of reparation. It was necessary for the children to console God and to ask pardon for those who do not believe, adore, or love Him. Secondly, the angel's requests were unique because they allowed for the children to exercise the common priesthood of all believers received in the Sacrament of Baptism by offering the reception of the Eucharist for those specific intentions. For Adele and the Fatima children, begging the Lord for the conversion of sinners through prayer, sacrifice, and offering Holy Communion became their lifelong ministry.

The Apparitions of Our Lady

Mary appeared in Fatima on the 13th of each month (with the exception of August, when the visionaries saw Our Lady on the

---

3   Miravalle, 865.
4   Miravalle, 865.

19th because they were imprisoned on the 13th), beginning in May and culminating in October, when the great miracle of the sun occurred.[5] In the first apparition, Our Lady asked the children if they would be willing to accept suffering in reparation for sin as an act of supplication for conversions. She also asked them to pray the rosary every day for world peace. In all, she basically reiterated the angel's requests for sacrifice and reparation. In the second apparition, on June 13th, Mary said that Jesus desired to establish a devotion to her Immaculate Heart in which salvation would be promised to the devotee. During July's apparition, she instructed the children to make sacrifices and taught them a prayer:

> Sacrifice yourselves for sinners, and say many times, especially whenever you make some sacrifice: "O Jesus, it is for love of you, for the conversion of sinners, and in reparation for the sins committed against the Immaculate Heart of Mary."[6]

The Blessed Mother also showed the children a vision of Hell and told them the current war was going to end. However, if people did not stop offending God, a worse war would break out. To this end, Our Lady stated that she would "ask for the conversion of Russia to [her] Immaculate Heart, and the Communion of Reparation on the First Saturdays."[7] Lastly, she taught what has come to be known as the Fatima Prayer, said after the Glory Be when reciting the rosary: "O my Jesus, forgive us our sins, save us from the fires of hell. Lead all souls to heaven, especially those who are most in need of thy mercy." In the fourth apparition on August 19th, Mary simply reiterated the children's mission to prayer, as, according to her, many souls go to Hell because no one prays or sacrifices for them. The fifth apparition emphasized the need to pray the rosary for world peace. In the sixth and final apparition, Our Lady revealed her name as the Lady of the Rosary. She added that people "must amend their lives and ask forgiveness for their sins."[8] Then St.

---

5   Miravalle, 874.

6   Miravalle, 871.

7   Miravalle, 872.

8   Miravalle, 876.

Joseph appeared with the child Jesus, and Mary appeared as Our Lady of Dolors and Our Lady of Mount Carmel. Following the apparition, the sun began to spin and cast multicolored light. Over 70,000 witnessed this miracle.

The First Five Saturdays

Following the Fatima apparitions, Francisco and Jacinta soon became victims of the influenza epidemic and died soon thereafter as Our Lady had revealed to them. Lucia entered the Sisters of Saint Dorothy and later entered a cloistered order of Carmelite sisters in Coimbra.[9] It was during her time as a Sister of St. Dorothy, on December 10, 1925, that Our Lady, with the Child Jesus, appeared to Lucia a seventh time. The devotion of the First Five Saturdays, which Mary had previously recommended during the third apparition, was further explained to Lucia. Lucia beheld the pierced and wounded Hearts of Jesus and Mary, which are pierced by blasphemies and ingratitude. Lucia was encouraged to make reparation through the First Saturday devotion. Those who "confess, receive Holy Communion, recite five decades of the Rosary and keep [Mary] company for fifteen minutes while meditation on the fifteen mysteries of the Rosary, with the intention of making reparation to [the Blessed Mother]" would be assisted at the hour of death and given the graces necessary for salvation.[10] Our Lady was thus relaying a specific formula in which reparation could be made. Just as Adele was told, in preparation for her mission, to make a general confession and offer her Communion for the conversion of sinners, Our Lady was preparing Lucia and countless others who have observed this tradition over the years. Mary was revealing her desire for the salvation of souls by calling souls to return to the sacraments, to prayer and contemplation. By going to the source of all strength, individuals would experience a conversion of their lives through the sacraments, and perhaps the fidelity of those Catholics who make reparation may encourage someone else to conversion and to make similar reparation. In both Champion and Fatima, Our Lady revealed a spirituality centered on the sacraments, specifically the Eucharist and Penance, which

---

9   Joseph A Pelletier, A.A., *Fatima: Hope of the World* (Worchester, MA: Washington Press, 1954), 131.

10   Miravalle, 878.

would result in personal conversion along with the intention of converting others.

Amendment of Life

In both Champion and Fatima, Our Lady asked that sinners do penance and amend their life. This is evident from her wish that the visionaries pray for the conversion of sinners and, in the case of Fatima, make reparation. In Champion, it is even more evident than Our Lady's conditional statement: "If they do not convert and do penance, my Son will be obliged to punish them". In Fatima Our Lady said:

> If people do not cease offending God, a worse [war] will break out during the pontificate of Pius XI. When you see a night illumined by an unknown light, know that this is the great sign given you by God, that he is about to punish the world for its crimes, by means of war, famine, and persecutions of the Church and the Holy Father.[11]

Mary came to warn the people that they must convert from their sinful ways. As seen in the language shift from Champion, which emphasized the sole need for prayer for the conversion of sinners, to Fatima's pressing need to make reparation, it seems that the world had entered into a moral decline in which a celestial intervention, that is an appearance of Mary, was necessary. All throughout the Fatima apparitions, Mary encouraged the children to pray the rosary for peace in the world. If the world did not want to see war, famine, and persecutions, people would have to turn away from sin, do penance, amend their lives, and pray, especially the rosary. If Mary's requests were heeded, war would be prevented. As with Champion, the so-called chastisement language does not necessarily need to be seen as a punishment inflicted upon the human race but rather as a natural result of man's lack of conversion. Famine results because of man's greed and selfishness, and persecutions of the Church arise out of man's personal ideologies. The remedy for these "punishments" due to sin is amendment of life and prayer, which Our Lady requested at both Champion and Fatima.

---

11   Miravalle, 872

Conclusion

At Fatima, Our Lady reiterated the message she had previously given to Adele. In this light, Fatima can be seen as a continuation of Champion in which Mary asks for personal conversion and a mission of prayer, reparation, and sacrifice for the conversion of sinners. The lives of Jacinta and Francisco were a testimony to suffering because they willingly took on suffering for the sake of conversions.[12] Lucia faithfully carried out her apostolate of prayer as a religious sister and most especially as a Carmelite nun later in life. Adele and the Fatima children remained faithful to what Our Lady had requested of them. The relevance of both apparitions is omnipresent in our society today, as evidenced by the continual moral decline and assault on the Catholic Church.[13] Throughout the centuries Mary has intervened at specific moments in history and spoken a message calling humankind to repentance. We must willingly respond to Our Lady's apostolate of prayer for the conversion of the world, which she requested at Champion and Fatima through the offering of Holy Communion. If we are faithful to Mary's request, perhaps what she had promised us at Fatima – world peace and the conversion of the world – will be obtained.

---

12   Francis Johnston, Fatima: *The Great Sign* (Washington, NJ: AMI Press, 1980), 101.

13   In the United States this is best exemplified by the assault on religious liberty which may force the closure of Catholic hospitals, universities, etc.

CHAPTER 13:
THE QUEEN OF HEAVEN:
A BELGIAN IMMIGRANT AND BELGIAN CHILDREN

Beginning on November 29, 1932 through January 3, 1933, five Belgian children, Fernande, Gilberte, and Albert Voisin; and Andrée and Gilberte Degeimbre, received a total of 33 apparitions of the Blessed Mother. Mary relayed exceptionally simple messages to each child, encouraging them to be good and to pray often. Throughout the apparitions Mary revealed to them her Golden Heart. In her final apparitions at Beauraing, Our Lady identified herself to one of the children as the Mother of God, the Queen of Heaven.

Since the apparitions of Beauraing, researchers and scholars have written about how the apparition served as a continuation or a fulfillment of previous Marian apparitions. Don Sharkey and Joseph Debergh, O.M.I. proposed that Beauraing is a sequel to Fatima.[1] H.M. Gillett relays the account of the Bishop of Tarbes and Lourdes who "publicly declared last summer in the pulpit at Lourdes: 'The cultus of Our Lady of Beauraing completes magnificently that of Lourdes ... Lourdes and Beauraing are the complements of one another."[2] As others have argued in the past for the complementarity of Beauraing and other such Mariophanies, the same can be said of Beauraing and Champion, perhaps even to a greater degree, given that the visionaries shared the same nationality and that Mary identified herself with the same name to Andrée as she did to Adele. Many similarities then are found between the two – the setting and description of Mary, the life situation, the message, the names, and the fact that each apparition served as a place of prayer at particular moments in history.

---

1   Joseph Debergh, O.M.I., *Our Lady of Beauraing* (Garden City, NY: Hanover House, 1958), 145.

2   H.M. Gillett, *Famous Shrines of Our Lady vol 1* (The Newman Press: Westminster, Maryland, 1952), 252.

The Apparition: Setting and Description of Mary

Even though great distances separate the two locales, Champion and Beauraing both share a common setting for each apparition, as they both occurred between or under one or more trees. In Champion, all three apparitions occurred at the same location – between a maple and a hemlock tree. During the sixth Beauraing apparition on December 1, 1932, Our Lady appeared "below the arched branch of the hawthorn tree."[3] For Beauraing, the setting is appropriate, as the city's name means "beautiful branch."[4] The same cannot be said for Champion. The maple and hemlock trees between which Mary appeared have no significance to the name of Champion. Spiritually, however, one could suggest the two trees represent the Tree of Life and the Tree of the Knowledge of Good and Evil.[5] Since Mary encouraged prayer for the conversion of sinners and catechesis of young people, individuals would be presented with two choices – whether to live only from the Tree of Life or to eat the bad fruit of the Tree of the Knowledge of Good and Evil. The choice was theirs – whether to accept Our Lady's request and be nourished by the Tree of Life or to ignore it and fall prey to the Tree of the Knowledge of Good and Evil. The hawthorn tree and the maple and hemlock trees are significant because it was Mary who chose to appear in these symbolic locations.

The pilgrims who come to the Shrine of Our Lady of Good Help after hearing the description of what Mary looked like during her appearance, question whether or not she would appear with long, golden, wavy hair. Their reaction is normal given the stereotypes associated with Jewish women. Jewish women are stereotypically characterized with darker hair and dark eyes. Mary's appearances to Adele and the Beauraing children are at odds with the stereotypical image of the Blessed Virgin as a traditional Jewish woman. In Beauraing, Gilberte said Our Lady had blue eyes.[6] While these two minute details, the color of Mary's hair and eyes, seem insignificant, they are extraordinarily revealing. In other apparitions, for example, Our Lady of Guadalupe and Our Lady of Kibeho, Our Lady appeared

---

3   Debergh, 46.
4   Debergh, 46.
5   C.f. Genesis 2:9 (RSV)
6   Debergh, 149.

in ways that would be familiar to the visionary or visionaries. Appearing in native Aztec dress, Our Lady and her message to Juan Diego became more appealing because the native people were more apt to accept her message as one of them. Would golden hair (characterized for our purposes as blonde) and blue eyes have been a familiar way for Our Lady to appear to the Belgian people? There is at least some acknowledgment of Belgians having blonde hair, as one of the parents, Marie Louise Perpete, is described as having blonde hair.[7] The way in which Mary appeared to Adele and the Beauraing visionaries suggests at the very least that in both apparitions, Mary appeared in a way in which she would not looked foreign. She instead appeared as one of them. She revealed herself to be a loving mother who wished to dialogue with her children, and in order to make the message acceptable, she appeared in a way familiar to the respective visionaries.

Lastly, there are similarities in Mary's attire. Adele described Mary as a

> beautiful lady, clothed in dazzling white, with a yellow sash around her waist. Her dress fell to her feet in graceful folds. She had a crown of stars around her head ... such a heavenly light shone around her that Adele could hardly look at her sweet face.[8]

The Beauraing children described Mary in a similar fashion but with some notable differences. In describing Our Lady's appearance, Gilberte answered:

> She wears a white dress shot with blue – as if it were reflecting something blue. The hem of her dress hides her feet and mingles with the white cloud on which she stands. Her hands are clasped together…She smiles and she has a white veil on her head which falls over her shoulders and comes nearly to her knees. There are rays of light all around her head, very straight and narrow.[9]

---

7   Debergh, 43.

8   Dominica, 8.

9   John Beevers, *The Golden Heart: The Story of Beauraing* (Chicago: Henry Regnery Company, 1956) 25.

The rays of light Gilberte described "formed a dazzling diadem for [Mary's] head".[10] Given the descriptions of Mary at Champion and Beauraing, Mary similarly wore a white dress, had rays of light surrounding her head, and wore a diadem or crown. At Champion, the white dress fell gracefully to Mary's feet, and in Beauraing the hem of her dress hid her feet. This white dress could be the symbol of Mary's purity. The crown which Mary wore symbolizes the name she revealed to the visionaries – the Queen of Heaven. As with the trees and Mary's blonde hair and blue eyes, these are simply factoids, yet they suggest similarities shared between the apparitions and set the scene for even greater similarities between Champion and Beauraing.

The purpose in showing the similarities is noteworthy, given that the apparitions were received by individuals of Belgian heritage. While Beauraing may be the completion of Lourdes and the sequel to Fatima, it shares much in common with Adele's apparition. Regardless of the apparitions' locations, Mary's appearance, and her apparel, these details emphasize continuity between Mary in her communication with the Belgian people, namely Adele and the five Beauraing children.

The Life Situation

Between Champion and Beauraing a general theme emerged for Mary's need to intervene at those specific moments in history, that is, spiritual apathy. The Belgian people's spiritual crisis due to the lack of a pastor was referenced several times in this book.[11] As a result, the Belgian immigrants to Northeastern Wisconsin fell away from the Church. The same was true for the Walloon population in Belgium, who "without being atheists, were far from being fervent Catholics."[12] In fact, Gilberte's family had not practiced their faith for a number of years, and her father, Hector, was known to frequently attend Socialist Party meetings.[13] Given the apparent spiritual crisis that was plaguing Belgium and even more specifically the Voisin family, the choice of Mary's place of appearance seemed appropriate to bring about a spiritual renewal within Belgium and the Voisin household.

---

10   Beevers, 17.

11   For further cross reference, see: Dominica, 3.

12   Debergh, 43.

13   Debergh, 43.

From the beginning, Mrs. Voisin wavered in her belief but mostly accepted the children's claims. She even encouraged them to pray and consult the parish priest, Fr. Leon Lambert. Later she even asked the priest to celebrate a Mass in honor of Mary so that a sign might be given that the apparitions were true.[14] Mary's appearance to the Beauraing children brought about a renewal of their families' faith, and as time would tell, throughout all of Belgium, as thousands would gather and pray at the apparition site.

While it is uncertain if the Brise family was practicing their faith (with the exception of Adele and her sister, Isabelle), or if they themselves had become prey to the spiritual crisis of the Northeastern Wisconsin Belgian settlement, what we do know is that Lambert and Catherine Brise accepted Adele's claims of visions. After the apparitions, her parents helped her in every way to ensure the message their daughter had received would be spread throughout the area. To Adele and the Beauraing children, Mary's apparitions occurred at a time people's faith needed renewal. It is amazing to realize that the claims of five children, alleging they saw the Blessed Mother, would bring thousands to the hawthorn tree in hopes of encountering the divine. Yet it was through these apparitions in Champion and Beauraing that the people's faith would be renewed and the faithful would have a new spiritual home in which they could make pilgrimages and request the Blessed Virgin's intercession. Of course, the purpose of Mary's apparition was not to glorify herself but to provide motherly guidance for her children so that they may experience the fullness of their faith in Christ Jesus. Her apparition brought the faithful back to the sacraments, reconciling them with the Church and providing lasting implications for their ultimate eternal destiny. It was out of love for the world that Mary appeared to Adele and the Beauraing children at a time of spiritual crisis.

The Message

The apparitions of Beauraing are unique in that Mary spoke to each individual child, either asking them a question or making an extremely simple statement. Like the Champion apparition, it could be said that Mary spoke in personal and general terms.

---

14   Debergh, 47, 48-9.

When she asked Fernande, "Do you love my Son? Do you love me?" Our Lady was asking her a personal question, but it was a question which could be asked of all who heard the story of the apparition. Thus, like the analysis of the Champion apparition in name, message, and mission, it could be said that Our Lady relayed a personal message and universal mission, namely to pray always. Beauraing's mission was simple because the visionaries themselves were simple; they were children. They were not yet at a state in life to work as Adele did, so their mission was simply to be good and pray always. This simple message nevertheless parallels that which Adele received.

On December 2, Our Lady instructed the children to "[a] lways be good."[15] She also asked them, "Is it true that you will always be good?" Mary was asking the children to amend their lives -- to no longer lie or talk back to their parents, but to live the commandments. However, this personal question encourages all people to consider the ways in which they offend God. A simple request to always be good means so much more. For Adele, it meant to go to Mass and receive the Sacrament of Penance, so as to turn away from sin in order to assist others in living the Christian life. To the children whom Adele catechized, she was telling them to always be good, as she showed them how to make the Sign of the Cross and taught them the faith. In Champion 70+ years earlier, Our Lady essentially gave the same instructions to Adele as she gave to the Beauraing children – always be good. This simple phrase can thus be seen as a continuation or a reminder to the Belgian children to live a life worthy of the gospel message.

The mission entrusted to the Beauraing children was quite simple: "Pray. Pray very much" and "Pray always." As a result, they were being called to a contemplative mission – to pray for the world and for one another. The children's mission of prayer was meant not only for them but also their families, the parish, and the greater community – the world at large. It is a simple reminder for the world to enter into silence and to commune with God. Again the message and mission of Beauraing can be seen as a simplification of the message and mission of Champion and

---

15   Debergh, 223. Subsequent quotations containing the dialogue Mary had with the Beauraing children should be assumed to have come from Appendix A of Debergh, p. 223-224.

rightly so since Our Lady was dialoguing with children. Adele's mission of prayer for the conversion of sinners was not to be a one-time affair; rather, it was something that she continuously kept before her since it was combined with her apostolic mission of catechizing. The mission of prayer was central to both Champion and Beauraing.

During the final apparition in Beauraing on January 3, 1933, Our Lady again asked a series of poignant questions to Fernande: "Do you love my Son? Do you love me?" Of course, Fernande said yes to each question. How could she not love Jesus and Mary, having been privileged to encounter Heaven on Earth? Our Lady's response to Fernande's answer was, "Then sacrifice yourself for me." Fernande was receiving a specific duty to sacrifice herself for Jesus and Mary. Mary did not specify the type of sacrifice required, so it could have meant self-sacrifice, or perhaps dedicating more time to prayer, or maybe even exerting herself to do more service to the Church and the community. The idea of sacrificing oneself could also be found in Adele's life and ministry. Our Lady asked Adele, "What are you doing here in idleness while your companions are working in the vineyard of my Son?" Following this question, Our Lady requested Adele to sacrifice herself by gathering the children and teaching them the Catholic faith. For Adele her sacrifice was to give her life away in order that the young and old alike would be able to hear the gospel message and have the means to amend their life. The questions Our Lady posed to Fernande and Adele could similarly be asked of us. We are called to think about what more we can do for the Lord. Do I pray enough? Do I own too much? Do I support the Church financially and through my own service? If not, then sacrifice yourself for Jesus, Mary, and the Church. Sacrifice your time, your treasure and give of your talent. Maybe your idleness can be remedied as Adele's was by instructing young people or through service at a local food pantry. You need only turn to Matthew 25, the Corporal Works of Mercy, or Catholic Social Teaching to find ways in which you can sacrifice yourself for the good of the Church and others.

During the apparitions in Champion and Beauraing, Our Lady spoke similar messages. Most interestingly, in the 33 apparitions of Our Lady at Beauraing, she did not always speak, she only revealed herself to the children. She abided with them and prayed with them. She revealed her Golden Heart. Similarly in Champion, Our Lady appeared three times, speaking only on the third time. Our Lady manifested herself quietly to Adele in order to prepare her. In both apparitions, the visionaries were called to deeper communion with Jesus and Mary through prayer and were told to amend their lives in different ways. The apparitions to the Beauraing children in 1932 and 1933 mirrors the apparitions Adele received in 1859. To the Belgians, Our Lady was giving a reminder that God exists and that they must live lives worthy of the kingdom, which meant to pray and to always be good. To this day, the message and mission entrusted to these visionaries continues through those who read or hear about the apparitions or make pilgrimages to those holy sites.

The Names of Mary

In the Mariophanies throughout history Mary has often revealed a specific name to the visionaries. A few examples include Lourdes (Immaculate Conception), Fatima (Lady of the Holy Rosary), and Kibeho, Africa (Mother of the Word). Apropos Beauraing, Our Lady identified herself by three names. She said, "I am the Immaculate Virgin" and, "I am the Mother of God, the Queen of Heaven." Two of these names, Immaculate Virgin and Queen of Heaven, will be addressed separately. Of most significance was Our Lady's revelation under the same title, the Queen of Heaven, to both Adele and to Andree. Thus, the names of Mary show a parallelism and continuity between these two apparitions.

Queen of Heaven

On October 9, 1859, Adele Brise, advised by her parish priest, asked Our Lady to identify herself in God's Name, to which she responded, "I am the Queen of Heaven who prays for the conversion of sinners." Over 70 years later, Our Lady, in her departing words to Andree at Beauraing, said, "I am the Mother of God, the Queen of Heaven; pray always." Mary's identification as the Queen of Heaven to both Adele and Andree is unique, given that both share a Belgian heritage. What is the significance of this identification? Historically, when Belgium declared independence from the Netherlands in 1830, the government decided to establish a constitutional monarchy.[16]   Similar to other monarchies, royalty was inherited within the royal family. The government appointed Leopold of Saxe-Coburg and Gotha as the first King of the Belgium.[17]   It would have been under Leopold I that the Brise family and many other Belgians decided to come to America. Similarly, the monarchy continued through the time of the Beauraing apparitions and up until today.

Mary's identification as the Queen of Heaven emphasizes the eternal kingdom (heaven) over our temporal kingdom (earth). Having come to America, the Brise family was liberated from the Belgian monarchy and welcomed a democratic government. Mary was telling Adele that she was the Queen and that she wanted her and others to be members of the celestial court. Even more importantly, it would only be a few years later in 1861 when the American Civil War would begin. As such, the Queen of Heaven title could also be seen as emphasizing that we should put no trust in princes (Psalm 146:3) but instead put our trust in the Son of Man – Jesus.[18]   Mary as the Queen of Heaven emphasizes that we as her children have a hereditary share in the eternal kingdom, if only we permit her to be our Queen so she may bring us to the King of Kings.

Similarly, in Beauraing, Mary's identification as the Queen of Heaven was emphasizing the same ideas, namely that the Belgian people must put their trust in Jesus. Given the spiritual apathy of the time, perhaps as a result of politics, Mary was calling the people to return to the Lord. In addition, the Beauraing apparition came shortly before the Second World War. The Queen of Heaven appellation emphasizes that all temporal rulers receive their power from the King par excellence, whether they accept that claim or not. The temporal kings have the power to do good or to misuse their power. Mary's reminder of the Eternal Monarchy came at an appropriate time in which the Belgian immigrants and citizens could rediscover their citizenship of heaven as rightful heirs of the King of Kings.

---

16   Cf. Emile Cammaerts, *Belgium: From the Roman Invasion to the Present Day* (Oakland: University of California Libraries, 1921), Chapter 24.

17   C.f. Henri Rolin, "The Constitutional Crisis in Belgium," *Foreign Affairs* 24.2, (Jan 1946), 300-303.

18   By this statement, I do not mean Our Lady was advocating for anarchy, but rather, that rulers of countries, because they are sinners, may not always have the Eternal Kingdom at the forefront of their decisions.

I will convert sinners

In appearing to Adele, Our Lady identified who she was and her role in salvation by describing herself as the Queen of Heaven who prays for the conversion of sinners. In her departing words to Gilberte, Our Lady told her that she would convert sinners. Seventy years later, Our Lady's language had changed. She originally said she prays for conversions, but in Beauraing she staunchly states she will convert sinners. Emil Neubert, SM, identified the work of Mary as a "Co-operatrix"[19] – one who works with Jesus in bringing about conversion, sanctification, and redemption.[20] Mary acknowledges her active role of prayer and work for conversions in cooperation with her Son's mission. The apparitions at Champion and Beauraing are like bookends. While in Champion, Adele cooperated in Our Lady's mission of praying and working for the conversion of sinners. Likewise, the prayers offered by the children of Beauraing as they heed Mary's instructions to pray always will assist her in her Co-operatrix role with her Son. Most importantly, Mary's identification and her mission as identified at Champion and Beauraing parallel each another in similar language. From this it seems that Our Lady was renewing the message and mission she once gave to a Belgian immigrant to another generation of Belgian children. Her message to Adele needed to be heard once again because of spiritual apathy and a decline in morality. Mary's message speaks of her cooperation in the work of her Son and her desire for the whole world to share in that mission. She did not speak simply in personal terms, even though at times her questions were personal in nature, but rather, she spoke with a universal mission of prayer and sacrifice for all those who hear the messages of Champion and Beauraing.

---

19   C.f. Emil Neubert, *My Ideal, Jesus, Son of Mary* (Charlotte: TAN Books, 2010), 84. This short devotional book was written as instructions from Jesus and Mary for the laity and is based on the spirituality of Fr. William Joseph Chaminade, the founder of the Marianists. Emil Neubert also wrote on the mission of Mary which would complement this understanding of Mary working with her Son for the salvation of souls. See: Emil Neubert, *Mary's Apostolic Mission and Ours* (New Bedford, MA: Academy of the Immaculate, 2011).

20   C.f. Lumen Gentium 56-65. The Second Vatican Council's Dogmatic Constitution on the Church also expounds on this notion.

I am the Immaculate Virgin

Besides Mary's identification as the Queen of Heaven to Andree, she also identified herself as the Immaculate Virgin. This name re-echoes Mary's identification as the Immaculate Conception, one who was preserved from original sin, but it also acknowledges that throughout her life, Mary remained sinless. The name is further intensified by what the children saw in a number of the apparitions – a golden heart.[21] The golden heart, coupled with Mary's identification as the Immaculate Virgin, results in a greater devotion to the Immaculate Heart. To have this devotion stem from the apparition is fitting, given that devotion to the Immaculate Heart was emphasized in the apparitions in Fatima and received by Lucia in the convent where the Five First Saturdays devotion was revealed. Mary's Immaculate Heart overflows with love for sinners, and her work of converting them flows from her love of God and love of her children. In addition, devotion to the Immaculate Heart was the fruit of Adele's apparition, as she received a picture of the Immaculate Heart to enshrine in the chapels, commemorating the apparition site.[22] More importantly, the Beauraing apparitions are commonly known as "The Golden Heart." This name, although unspoken but yet revealed within Mary's appearance, is similar to Champion since that apparition is also known by a devotional name rather than the identification of Mary to Adele. The names and roles attributed to Mary at the given apparitions parallel one another quite nicely and reveal Beauraing to be a continuation or a renewal of the message once spoken to a Belgian immigrant many years earlier.

Places of Pilgrimage

During several apparitions, including Lourdes and Fatima, Mary instructed the visionaries to request the local bishop to build a chapel at the site of the apparition. This is notable because it again highlights Mary's desire to always bring people to her Son. The same was true at Beauraing – Our Lady said she desired a chapel to be built so that pilgrims could visit the site of her apparition. This request, however, was absent from

---

21   The description of Mary's Golden Heart as seen by the children can be found in Beevers, 37-38.

22   C.f. Dominica, 9.

the dialogue Adele had with Mary. Regardless of its absence, immediately following the apparition in Champion, chapels were indeed built, and eventually each chapel needed to be replaced to accommodate the growing numbers of visitors. The significance of Champion and Beauraing as places of pilgrimage rests with the fact that each placed a pivotal role at specific moments in history. In 1871 the chapel became a refuge of prayer when people gathered there the night of the Peshtigo Fire. Their prayer at the site of Mary's apparition exemplified their trust and devotion to Our Lady, and as a result, their lives were spared. Just as those in the Belgian settlement flocked to the chapel that night, similarly on May 10, 1940

> German airplanes filled the skies over the eastern part of Belgium. ...Bombs were dropped on cities and airports. ...Panic swept the residents of Beauraing as the German troops approached. On May 11 most of the inhabitants packed their belongings and started toward the French border. They went on foot, on bicycle, by horse cart, and by automobile. German bombers roared overhead. Many of the people stopped at the hawthorn and lighted vigil candles before they left the city. Beauraing was almost deserted. Only 129 people were left out of a population of two thousand.[23]

While the citizens of Beauraing did not take refuge at the hawthorn tree, they did, however, make a pious stop to ask the Virgin's intercession and protection during wartime. It was reported that the rosary at Beauraing continued even with so few people in the town, illustrating the Queen of Heaven's continued intercession.[24] On September 7, 1944, when American tanks rolled into Beauraing, marking the end of the enemy occupation, the residents went to the apparition site to offer their gratitude to Mary.[25] Also signifying their gratitude, "twenty thousand freshly liberated prisoners of war made a pilgrimage to Beauraing on October 14, 1945, to thank the Virgin for their return to their

---

23   Debergh, 195-6.
24   Debergh, 196.
25   Debergh, 202.

homeland and their families."[26] The place of Mary's apparition was a place for prayers of intercession and thanksgiving during this turbulent time for the Belgian people. Individuals were able to take solace in their prayers at an apparition site. The same can be said of Champion; following the Peshtigo Fire, the annual celebration of the Assumption saw a significant increase in attendance from people who were just beginning to accept Adele's claims following that horrific event.[27] Both apparition sites, then, served as a place of refuge for those who wanted to exhibit their faith and devotion to Our Lord and Blessed Lady.

Banneux

Given the similarities of Champion and Beauraing, one would be remiss not to acknowledge the other approved apparition which occurred several days following the conclusion of the Beauraing apparition. Beginning on January 15, 1933 and ending on March 2 of that same year, Our Lady appeared to a girl named Mariette Beco, who was 11 years old. The visionary's family situation was similar to those of Beauraing and the settlement at Champion – "Her father [was] a hard working laborer and a badly-lapsed Catholic."[28] As a result of Mary's apparition, her father was reconciled with God through the Sacrament of Penance. Mary's appearance in dress was similar to Champion, for Mariette saw a woman dressed in a long white robe which hung to her feet. Mary wore a blue girdle (instead of a yellow sash at Champion) and "rays of light shone from her head."[29] The apparition's message was also quite simple: Mary desired a chapel to be built and encouraged Mariette to pray hard. To those Belgians who saw Mary (and also in other apparitions), Our Lady emphasized the necessity of prayer. Our Lady identified herself as the Virgin of the Poor, and the spring of water at Banneux was set apart for all the nations but especially the sick, as Mary had come to relieve the sick.[30] The Banneux apparition, like Lourdes, involves a healing spring. But Mary's indication of her action or mission, that of relieving the sick, parallels with the spiritual sickness

---

26   Debergh, 202.
27   Dominica, 32.
28   Gillett, 260.
29   Gillett, 263.
30   Gillett, 264.

during Adele's time and now at the time of the apparitions in Beauraing and Banneux. Following the apparition, a hospital was built at Banneux to fully carry out Mary's desire of relieving the sick. This, of course, is similar to the chapel and convent built as a means for Adele to catechize the young people. Like Champion and Beauraing, Our Lady appeared at Banneux with a specific purpose of encouraging a young girl to remain faithful to prayer and to establish a place of healing for the entire world.

Conclusion

The apparitions received by Adele, the five children at Beauraing, and Mariette at Banneux all reiterate the same message and desire of Mary – to bring people closer to her Son. To the Belgian people she appeared at appropriate times in which the faith needed to be renewed, and she appeared in similar places wearing similar attire. The messages and missions entrusted to the respective visionaries should not be seen in isolation from one another but as a continuation, renewal, and fulfillment of each another. It is appropriate that Adele's Mariophany was a bit more in-depth, for Adele was much older than the Beauraing children and Mariette. Mary's messages at Beauraing and Banneux further help to bring Champion's message to the Belgian people. Reminding people of their heavenly destiny, Mary, she who is the Immaculate Virgin, the Golden Heart, the Queen of Heaven, and Virgin of the Poor, came to remind people that God exists and that they should live according to His commandments. Each apparition site has become a place of intercession in which the story of the respective vision may be passed on to future generations. Our Lady's overall message to the Belgian people is not archaic; it always remains relevant.

CONCLUSION:
BLESSED ARE THEY WHO
BELIEVE WITHOUT SEEING

In 2010, Bishop David L. Ricken released a decree on the authenticity of Adele's apparitions. In that decree, he emphasized that the apparitions were deemed worthy of belief, although not obligatory among the Christian faithful. In 1859, two young women accompanied Adele and knelt at her command, to which the Queen of Heaven responded, "Blessed are they who believe without seeing," quoting John 20:29. Those young women believed Adele because she had no reason to lie to them. They knelt and as such were commended for their faith. Today, over 150 years later, people still come to the humble Shrine of Our Lady of Good Help because they accept the testimony of a 28-year-old Belgian immigrant who claimed she saw Mary. They come with heavy hearts and with special intentions. Some are unemployed and are seeking employment; others have terminal diseases like cancer; still others are seeking a cure for other health problems.

Over the years countless pilgrims have described feeling a quaint and serene presence at the site where Mary appeared. People light hundreds of candles throughout the property as a sign that their prayer continues after they leave. Like those two women who knelt at Adele's command and received that affirmation from Mary, Mary says the same thing to all of us today. She says, Blessed are you who come to this holy place, who pray and light candles, all because you believe Adele's testimony expressed by the way she responded to God's call in her life. Her belief in the message and mission transformed her life and in effect transformed the lives of all those to whom she ministered.

Like Adele, we too are being called by the Lord, and prayed for by Our Lady, to participate in this special mission of passing on the Catholic faith to our loved ones. We are being called to pray for the conversion of sinners, to go to Mass and receive the Eucharist, and to go to confession. We are being asked to teach the faith to others. The way in which each of us lives out the message will be different. Maybe those who read this will sign up to be a catechist at their parish. Or parents and grandparents might take their children or grandchildren to church or read a story from the bible or about the saints. Others might pray before they eat, even at school or work, and perhaps a friend or co-worker will see their love and devotion to the faith, and maybe they will think about God for the first time in a while. Perhaps an old cliché best illustrates this point: "You might be the only bible a person ever reads." Our joy, love, and devotion to the Lord should be so contagious that those who encounter us should be moved to faith and love of Jesus and the Church. Adele's life should inspire us, her personal message should cause us to reflect on our own life, and her mission of prayer and catechesis should inspire us to do the same. By the intercession of Mary, the Queen of Heaven and Our Lady of Good Help, and under the inspiration of Adele, may we in the third millennium be inspired to grow in our faith and witness it to those around us. May the work of the new evangelization under Our Lady's patronage grant a renewal of the faith in our world today. Amen.

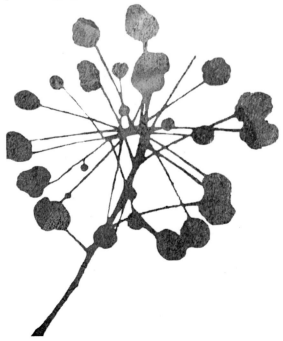

SIDES OF THE SAME COIN:
ST. ANGELA MERICI AND SISTER ADELE BRISE

On January 27th the Catholic Church celebrates the memorial of St. Angela Merici, an Italian saint. The story of St. Angela Merici's life bears some resemblance to the story of a Belgain immigrant to the United States, Adele Brise. In 1859, the Blessed Mother appeared to Adele, exhorting her to teach the young people their catechism, how to sign themselves and what they needed to know for salvation. On December 8, 2010, Bishop David Ricken, declared with moral certainty, although not obligatory, that the apparitions received by Adele Brise were worthy of belief.

Below are some similarities between St. Angela and Sister Adele:

* St. Angela was the founder of the Ursaline order. Sister Adele was instructed by the Ursaline Sisters in Belgium and had a great desire to enter their congregation. At a young age Adele and a few of her friends entered into a pact to join the Ursalines.[1] Adele, however, immigrated to the United States and this dream was never realized.

* St. Angela was blind in one eye but was cured after a pilgrimage to the Holy Land. Adele was also blind in one eye. Unlike St. Angela, there is no record of Adele's healing from that physical ailment.

* St. Angela was a tertiary of St. Francis and Sister Adele founded a lay group of Franciscan tertiares who taught young people their catechism. A school was later built at the property of the Shrine of Our Lady of Good Help.

* Both St. Angela and Adele were granted heavenly visions. Although St. Angela's sister died without the sacraments, Angela was granted a vision of her sister in the company of the saints in Heaven. Adele was granted a vision of the Queen

---

1   This fact has been speculated but never confirmed.

of Heaven.

* St. Angela had another vision later in life in which she was told to form a community of virgins who were to dedicate their lives to teaching. Adele founded a lay group of sisters, dedicated to teaching, in order to fulfill the request of Our Lady to gather the children and teach them their catechism.

* Both had a great desire to teach the young people! St. Angela was "Convinced that the great need of her times was a better instruction of young girls in the rudiments of the Christian religion, she converted her home into a school where at stated intervals she daily gathered all the little girls of Desenzano and taught them the elements of Christianity" (New Advent). Adele founded a group of lay sisters to teach on the chapel (now shrine) property, fulfilling the message given to her. Later, Adele's dwindling order was assumed by the Bay Settlement Sisters, who staffed schools in the Diocese of Green Bay.

* Lastly, each wrote letters to the families of students. An example of St. Angela's is provided in the Office of Readings (Proper of Saints) found in the four volume Liturgy of the Hours for her feast. Similarly, the Diocese of Green Bay Archives has copies of correspondences between Adele and families, in which she shared the story of the apparition, an update on their son or daughter, and a request for tuition payment.

In comparing the lives of St. Angela Merici, who was born in 1470 and died in 1540, to the life of Adele Brise, of the 1800's, it can be seen that both share commonalities in their life and vocational paths. From physical problems to visions they both shared a similar mission; you could say they are two sides of the same coin.

ACKNOWLEDGEMENTS:

I would like to thank those people who have helped me in a special way to prepare this book for publication:

To Dave Conger for his diligent effort in editing my original manuscript.

To *America Magazine* and Fr. James Martin for permission to reproduce his article on the connections between Lourdes and Champion.

To the Mariological Society of America for their permission to reproduce my presentation which will be published at a later time in their 2011 journal Marian Studies.

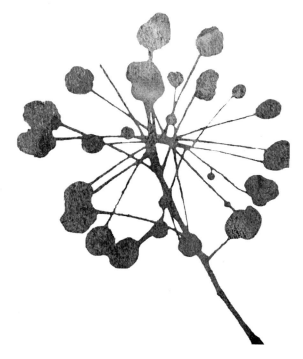